Reviving the Church in America

Copyright © 2023 by Chris Sonksen

Published by Arrows & Stones

All rights reserved. No portion of this book may be reproduced, stored in a retrieval system, or transmitted in any form or by any means—electronic, mechanical, photocopy, recording, scanning, or other—except for brief quotations in critical reviews or articles, without prior written permission of the author.

Unless otherwise noted, all Scriptures are from the Holy Bible, New International Version®, NIV®. Copyright © 1973, 1978, 1984, 2011 by Biblica, Inc.™ Used by permission of Zondervan. All rights reserved worldwide. www.zondervan.com. The "NIV" and "New International Version" are trademarks registered in the United States Patent and Trademark Office by Biblica, Inc.™ | Scripture quotations marked MSG are taken from THE MESSAGE, copyright © 1993, 1994, 1995, 1996, 2000, 2001, 2002 by Eugene H. Peterson. Used by permission of NavPress. All rights reserved. Represented by Tyndale House Publishers, Inc. | Scripture quotations marked NKJV are taken from the New King James Version®. Copyright © 1982 by Thomas Nelson. Used by permission. All rights reserved. | Scripture quotations marked NLT are taken from the Holy Bible, New Living Translation, copyright © 1996, 2004, 2015 by Tyndale House Foundation. Used by permission of Tyndale House Publishers, Inc., Carol Stream, Illinois 60188. All rights reserved. |

For foreign and subsidiary rights, contact the author.

Cover design by Sara Young
Cover photo by Brenton Stanley

ISBN: 978-1-960678-68-3   1 2 3 4 5 6 7 8 9 10

Printed in the United States of America

11 Testimonials from the
Church Rescue Movement

Reviving the Church in America

Chris Sonksen

ARROWS & STONES

Contents

Introduction 7

1   Charles Scheffe 17

2   Rob Shepherd 27

3   Seth Dee 33

4   Tony Orlando 41

5   Dan Zemlicka 45

6   Alex Lara 55

7   Vinny Greene 67

8   Dan Edwards 79

9   Bryan Hallmark 93

10   Charles Olmeda 105

11   Joel Wood 119

The Sleeping Giant 131

Introduction

You've received this book because you've joined the movement. In fact, I believe this is one of the most important movements in recent history. Do you think I'm overstating the point? Let me explain:

In 2021, I met with fifteen pastors in Dallas. They lead fairly large churches from several different denominations and all parts of the country. We were concerned about the state of the church in the United States, and we wanted to pool our insights and resources to see if we could do something about it. These leaders had been blessed by the organization I started in 2016 called Church Boom, and they wanted to pay the blessing forward. We'd all heard the statistics because they'd been broadcast on CNN and Fox and described in articles in America's premier newspapers. Let me cite a few. Research expert Thom Ranier observed: "Eight out of ten of the approximately 400,000 churches in the United States are declining or have plateaued," and "84 percent are declining or experiencing a growth rate below the population growth rate for their communities. The latter is defined as a plateaued church."[1]

Pew Research found that as of 2020, 64 percent of Americans identify as Christians, down from 90 percent five decades ago.[2] But a lot of those who claim to be believers don't go to church. *The Washington Post* has an article titled, "Church membership has dropped below the majority for the first time in nearly a century."[3]

According to Lifeway Research, approximately 4,500 churches closed their doors in 2019 (the latest year with accurate records) and only 3,000 new churches opened.[4]

The other pastors and I realized America was becoming like Europe, with a lot of big church buildings and very, very few people attending on any Sunday. Mosques are growing in number and attendance more than Christian churches! A church leader responded to this alarming trend: "We can no longer simply ignore struggling

---

[1] Thom Ranier, *Breakout Churches* (Grand Rapids: Zondervan, 2005).
[2] Sarah McCammon, Michael Levitt, and Kathryn Fox, "America's Christian Majority is Shrinking, and Could Dip Below 50% by 2070," *NPR*, September, 15 September 2022, https://www.npr.org/2022/09/15/1123289466/americas-christian-majority-is-shrinking-and-could-dip-below-50-by-2070.
[3] Sarah Pulliam Bailey, "Church Membership Has Dropped Below the Majority for the First Time in Nearly a Century," *Washington Post*, 29 March 2021, https://www.washingtonpost.com/religion/2021/03/29/church-membership-fallen-below-majority/.
[4] Aaron Earl, "Protestant Church Closures Outpace Openings in U.S.," *Lifeway Research*, 25 May 25 2021, https://research.lifeway.com/2021/05/25/protestant-church-closures-outpace-openings-in-u-s/.

INTRODUCTION

churches. We must give attention to these churches before they die or we all lose!"[5]

These dismal statistics—and this heart for the American church—prompted us to meet in Dallas. As we talked, two principles emerged. First, "revelation requires responsibility". If these numbers are true (and they are), what can be done about it? The Bride of Christ is in the ER, and she needs our help! And second, the decline of the American church is happening "on our watch". We wondered what we would say when we stood before God to give an account of our leadership and He asked, "If you knew all this, why didn't you do something about it?"

We asked ourselves, "What if . . .?" What if we provide encouragement, resources, and support to turn these churches around? What if we devote some of what God has given us to those pastors and churches so that they can thrive? We focused on churches of less than one hundred people, and our goal was to help them grow beyond one hundred. We decided to call it "Church Rescue". As we talked, God gave us a four-fold strategy:

---

[5] Dr. Aubrey Malphurs, "The State of the American Church: Plateaued or Declining," *Malphurs Group*, https://malphursgroup.com/state-of-the-american-church-plateaued-declining/.

Reviving the Church in America

- Coaching—We made commitments to coach pastors of struggling churches for a year in groups of eight to ten on Zoom, free of charge. If they wanted to go further, we offered a second year. Quite often, leaders of declining and plateaued churches have lost their sense of mission because they're so worried about just keeping the doors open. We wanted to refresh their vision and encourage them to believe God for more... much more.

- Resources—We realized these churches needed as much training and help as we could provide. So, we began creating podcasts, blogs, and live leadership training events free of charge.

- Financial help—Funding is always a challenge for churches that are underwater, so we committed to providing emergency financial assistance. Some are behind in rent, some have leaky roofs, and others have toilets that don't flush. (We've paid for repairs for things you might never imagine!) It's very hard for people in a church to invite friends and neighbors to a church where they don't feel comfortable... or even safe.

INTRODUCTION

- Soul care retreat—We created and funded a four-day, all-expenses-paid retreat for the pastors so they could experience uninterrupted time with God, the encouragement of trusted leaders, and the loving bond of a community.

We asked healthy churches to provide resources for unhealthy ones, and business leaders caught the vision, too. We created "Rescue Sundays" to present the concept to congregations who might want to contribute to this cause, and we held our first event in August of 2021 at Mosaic Church in Sacramento, California, led by pastor Jeff Seaman. We weren't sure how people in the congregation would respond, but they immediately caught the vision and made commitments to give to the movement.

We soon realized one of our challenges is that rescuing churches isn't sexy. We couldn't show pictures of water wells dug in Africa or hungry children being fed in Latin America. (We thought about showing fixed toilets, but the idea didn't go very far.) We were concerned that some people might hear about the problem and assume the best solution is Darwin's: the survival of the fittest! But our fears weren't realized. When people hear the statistics and realize the fate of the church is at stake,

Reviving the Church in America

they gladly join us. At these events, I almost invariably tell people, "Go home and Google 'American churches closing' and see what comes up. You'll be astounded. You'll also realize the problem is almost certainly much worse than you thought."

Why does this movement matter? What difference will it make? Here's the point: rescued churches rescue people, and rescued churches can also rescue America. As each set of church doors closes, America gets a little darker. Our movement's goal is to keep lights burning and help them burn much brighter in communities all over the country.

When I speak at Rescue Sundays, I often ask, "How many of you would say, 'We're not the same country we were twenty years ago?'" And lots of hands go up. Then I ask, "How many of you would say, 'We're not the same country we were just two or three years ago?'" I see a lot of wide-eyed realization that the pace of decline in our nation is speeding up. It's time to do something about it! I then explain, "Folks, we have a couple of choices: we can complain and point fingers, or we can fight for the only sources of hope, truth, grace, and love in many communities in our land. I believe the local church is the hope of America. Which will you choose?"

INTRODUCTION

In Luke 10:27-37 (NLT), Jesus told the religious leaders a story that applies to us today. One of the leaders heard Jesus say that the greatest commandment is to love God and love our neighbors, and he asked, "Who is my neighbor?" (I'm pretty sure he wanted Jesus to narrow the scope of who might qualify.) In response, Jesus told a stunning story that began, "A Jewish man was traveling from Jerusalem down to Jericho, and he was attacked by bandits. They stripped him of his clothes, beat him up, and left him half dead beside the road." Two Jewish leaders walked by the scene, but they didn't offer the man any assistance at all. "Then a despised Samaritan came along, and when he saw the man, he felt compassion for him. Going over to him, the Samaritan soothed his wounds with olive oil and wine and bandaged them. Then he put the man on his donkey and took him to an inn, where he took care of him. The next day he handed the innkeeper two silver coins, telling him, 'Take care of this man. If his bill runs higher than this, I'll pay you the next time I'm here.'"

Jesus asked the Jewish leader, "Now which of these three would you say was a neighbor to the man who was attacked by bandits?"

Reviving the Church in America

The leader responded, "The one who showed him mercy."

Jesus told him, "Yes, now go and do the same."

I want to draw two principles from this passage: First, *notice the need right in front of you*. The irony of the story is that the hero is a man who seems to be the most unlikely of all. The Samaritan had no status, no clout, and was not even welcomed in Israel, but he noticed someone in need when others walked on by. And second, *do what you can with what you have*. To carry the wounded man, the Samaritan probably needed a horse, but all he had was his donkey. He did what he could with what he had. He probably needed to take the man to a hospital, but the inn would have to do. The beaten man may have needed real medicine instead of oil and wine, but he did what he could with what he had.

These are the principles that are driving the Church Rescue movement. When people notice the need, they're eager to get involved. And we're not asking them to give a million dollars; we're only asking them to do what they can with what they have.

INTRODUCTION

As you'll see in the stories in this book, God is using people just like you to make a huge difference in the lives of pastors and the health of churches. In hundreds of places in the country, the light is shining much brighter!

1

Charles Scheffe

How do you get to the point of needing rescue? That is a great question. And not one that is always easy to answer. Perhaps after the autopsy, many can see all the signs. And now looking back, I can see many of my own. But I got to a point that things just had to change. They could not stay the same. God had not called me nor my family for things to be like they were. It did not happen suddenly—well, most of it anyway. It was not one singular thing that got us into a bad place. And like most things, it was a series of decisions that kept me and our church stuck. So, what happened?

Reviving the Church in America

Let me start with this—we are a church plant. We started with only three people, and it parachuted into a new community almost six years ago. Things were going well. In the first two and a half years, we baptized thirty people. We grew from three to over one hundred with 175 on Christmas Eve, and we had plans for an even stronger Easter 2020. Then a pandemic hit. COVID-19 devastated the world, took many lives, and also took many churches that failed to survive. I have been in ministry for over twenty years, and I have never experienced anything like it. I would dare say that most of us in ministry during that time carry a wound, battle scar, or even worse from that season of ministry. We were a young church, still growing, and in a week, we were stripped of a location that was large enough to house our growing 120 people (a local school). But we lost much more than our location. We lost our vision and methodology of doing church. We believe that the church does three things: gathers, grows, and goes. And it was fundamental to our DNA. We gathered weekly in a local school. We were growing in groups that met in homes across our community. We did events for our community, school, and more. I'd like to believe that we were a force in our local community. And we were doing all three of those things, until the day the school called and said we could not meet there any longer. That was

CHARLES SCHEFFE

a fun phone call on a Thursday afternoon. We only had one choice that coming Sunday—to go online. But we were a physical church with a little digital footprint. We had some online and digital experience, but at the time, we thought it was more important to continue investing in other places because the online option would "come eventually." We attempted to livestream a service from inside my living room that first Sunday—fifteen people crammed into a 20x20 space with cameras, lights, keyboards, TVs, and wires everywhere. Needless to say, it was a disaster. We had to pare down our team to be more functional and create a way for people to still connect at least for the next few weeks. We killed a few teams, like First Impressions, which were designed to engage new guests when they came onto our campus, and we brought on a new team member who was experienced in the social media world and adapted quickly to learning the art of production with an eye for what we needed to communicate to the world around us. And she was instrumental in our survival.

That next few weeks became a few months and before you know it—over a year. We went from a church that was gathering weekly in person, growing in groups, and serving our community to a church that was online only. Yes, we weren't able to meet in person for over a year.

Reviving the Church in America

You might be wondering to yourself, *surely there was somewhere they could have met*. We tried just about everything. We exist in a bedroom community that has a single grocery store, a McDonald's, a Taco Bell, and a Walgreens. Everything was brand new and built to suit, so there were no spaces to rent or buy, and the building was still an answer 18+ months out. We were stuck. We even met outdoors in local parks, and at 110+ degrees in Phoenix, that becomes its own challenge. HOA even made new rules for us because of the things we tried. We laughed about it all at the time—if they aren't making rules about you, then you are not trying. But the truth was ... we were dying.

Fast forward through those thirteen months, and by the grace of God and because of His purpose, we survived the pandemic—perhaps only barely. But everything shifted during that year: our process, our outreach, and our ability to recruit, build, and encourage leaders. And I am not sure we knew how much we had lost until eighteen months after coming back.

Everyone wanted so badly to get back to in-person gatherings. And they were right. We needed it. We needed each other. But everyone still had the picture of this pre-pandemic church that we once were. But we were no longer that church. On Easter of 2021, we relaunched but this time with a broken vision, little preparation, and missing leadership—and leadership that was tooled for a different task entirely. It was like trying to fly a plane while constructing it in midair with duct tape as your best tool.

In his book, *Good to Great,* Jim Collins says, "You need the right people in the right seats on your bus."[6] And a few months after coming back, I wasn't sure if we even had the right bus. The guy who started the church with me left. And the gal that had been so critical during COVID seemed like she was fighting with everyone in the church. And I was at the center of it all. I could not see any path forward.

So, in the first week of January, I called a friend of mine, Jackie Allen. Jackie is a successful pastor and someone I have looked up to for quite a while. And I felt just like Jackie—I couldn't keep going like this or the direction that we were headed in. I wasn't even sure which way was up. The church was floundering. We had spiked a few good Sundays, but in reality, we were not growing. We were a flat one hundred, at best. We had not baptized anyone in eight months. And all I saw

---
6 Jim Collins, *Good to Great: Why Some Companies Make the Leap . . . and Others Don't* (HarperBusiness, 2001).

was conflict. I was spiritually, emotionally, and even mentally drowning. Jackie said "Let's get you a coach. Someone who can walk through where you are with you, point out what needs to be addressed, and what steps to take. And Jackie so believed in the power of such a coach that he said, "I will split the cost with you." Of course, I responded, "Deal! I am in! I just need something different because what I am doing right now is not working." I was not going to let this new year be the same as the past year.

It took almost two weeks before Pastor Chris and I met. And those two weeks felt like an eternity! I was excited, nervous, and sort of unsure what this process would be like. Sure, I had coaches in high school and college, but those were for athletics. What would this be like?

The day that Pastor Chris and I met, I remember thinking, *just don't sound stupid. This guy is going to be with you for the whole year—you will have plenty of time for that. This is just a meet and greet and some fluff.* And we did exactly that. Our conversation went a little like this: here is my story; here is your story. Let's do this together, rah rah rah. It was good. We got to the end of our conversation, and everything was fine. And by fine, I mean the church was still burning, and I was just sitting sipping coffee kind of fine. Then Pastor Chris asked me about my team. I must have flinched. Because he said, "Uh oh." And within the next ten minutes, I poured out the conflict that was underlying everything in our church. And Pastor Chris looked at me and said, "You have to deal with this. You can either pay now or pay later. But make no mistake, you will pay." And he began to lay out a conflict resolution process with a heart of restoration for our church, my leader, and me. It was biblical and came straight out of Matthew 18. Pastor Chris laid out the steps:

Step 1. You need to get face-to-face with this leader.

Step 2. You need to very clearly state what you have observed and how that is affecting everything.

Step 3. You need to listen. This might be the hardest part. And thankfully, Pastor Chris said as much. He said this is a moment when you have to get as much of the ick out or it will never get resolved.

Step 4. You have to move forward.

Now it was getting real!

Reviving the Church in America

I took what Pastor Chris suggested and chewed on it for the next two days. My thought was, *this is going to suck*. But he was right. I had let it get to a point that my leader was not just questioning where we were going but was even questioning who was leading. And if there are only two of us, which at the time there was, then we had to fix it. There were only two choices: We fix us and move forward, or we separate and move forward. Both choices would have the same effect on the church—it would move forward.

That meeting was gross and hard with lots of tears. And even after the meeting, I was not sure which of the two solutions we were taking. I texted Pastor Chris afterward and shared my thoughts again. He was just a bouncing board more than anything at that moment. A week later, my leader came back. She believed in the mission of the church, and she believed in me as a leader. And we took that and used that as a building block and changed her seat on the bus.

Four weeks later, we started baptizing again. We baptized three people in a young family who had come the Sunday after our meeting. Wow, God is so good. And He often is waiting for us to be obedient so that he can do the work and the plans that He already has in store.

CHARLES SCHEFFE

Easter was a few weeks after that, and we held two services. We had tried two services before, but that sort of fell flat for lots of reasons. This time was different. We had what would have been a normal service first, and then a max capacity service following that. We had over 300 people—yes, we tripled what we had been running in the fall! And we had more baptisms. We baptized seven more people. In those ten weeks, we baptized ten people, and we had four more people say yes to Jesus in our Easter service, including my six-and-a-half-year-old daughter.

Through the summer—which is supposed to be a slower season for baptisms in Phoenix—we averaged 125 people, saw three more salvations, added a new full-time pastor to our staff, and are now making plans and leading our service teams toward the launch of a second service set to start in January. Grasp all that for just a second. While in conflict, the church was suffering and floundering, my team member was suffering, and so was I. One year later, we are looking at adding a second service because our first service is full—not because we love the idea of two (although it has some advantages)—but because to be obedient and reach more people, we have to have it! God is good. God requires our obedience.

Rob Shepherd

I never dreamed church planting would be so difficult. I had fifteen years of ministry experience and the last eight were at a fast-growing megachurch before I planted my own church. I have a degree in Youth Ministry and a Master of Divinity. I'm not sure how you master the Divine, but I had a degree to prove I had done it. While on church staff, I was well-liked, often the peacemaker, and praised for my creativity. Six months into planting a church, it seemed like no one liked me, and my creativity was being criticized. Something changes when you are the lead pastor, and the decisions rise and fall on you. I felt a heavy burden, and I felt alone. I needed some guidance and help.

We had over one hundred people coming that first year, but it seemed like there was constant conflict. A lot of the conflict was with staff and leadership. There was misalignment and challenges everywhere I looked. I was in over my head and needed help. I thought that all I needed to do was cast vision and people would follow. I never dreamed that the very vision I thought was coming from God would be questioned and criticized.

One of my best friends was on staff for a large leadership conference. He has everyone's cell phone number and is very well connected. He came to the town where I live, and we connected over dinner. I'll never forget pouring my heart out to him that night. He asked how the church was doing and after sharing some wins, I unloaded the struggles I was feeling on him. I told him specifically because I was hoping he could help me find some coaching. I told him about how I sought out a few coaching networks and they all seemed the same. They were very expensive and seemed to offer an impersonal experience. Basically, you pay for a big-name pastor to share some insight or vision with a group of ten to fifteen other pastors. I was looking for something more personal and affordable. I needed to meet with someone who I could share my specific issues with and receive their coaching. I didn't want a cookie-cutter coaching network. I needed someone who could hear what I was dealing with and give me insight to help me fix the issues. My friend said that the type of coaching I was looking for did not exist. I left that meeting committed to praying for a ministry coach. I believed that God was limited by my lack of resources. I never dreamed that God could answer those prayers the way that He did.

Fast forward six months later, and that same friend I met with over dinner invited me to go on a vision trip to Haiti with eleven other pastors. It was a chance to learn about a great organization that is making a difference in the lives of Haitian orphans. I immediately said "yes" and the next thing I knew, I was in Haiti. My friend was also on the trip but he was not the leader of the trip. The leader was some guy named Chris Sonksen and he was stuck in an airport in Dallas, TX. It seemed like all the other pastors knew who Chris was. They were excited for him to get to Haiti.

On the second day of the trip, Chris Sonksen shows up. He had so much energy and positivity, especially coming from someone who had just slept in an airport all night.

Reviving the Church in America

I had a few conversations with Chris, but with eleven other pastors there, I didn't get a lot of time to connect with him. I knew he was a very well-connected pastor and author but I didn't know much else about him. The trip ended, and I went back home to my church.

A few weeks after that trip to Haiti, I got a call from Chris Sonksen. He said that he has a heart for church planters and would love to come speak at my church, and then coach my team afterward. I was incredibly honored but quickly let him know that we didn't have any money for a guest preacher or coaching. Chris says, "Oh, you misunderstood me. I was offering to come on my dime." Before I knew it, Chris Sonksen was preaching to my church and coaching my staff. It was incredible! The next day my staff was energized and asked if we could get more coaching from Chris and ChurchBOOM. I reached out to Chris, and we immediately started receiving coaching from ChurchBOOM. This was what I had been praying for and desperately needed. ChurchBOOM offered coaching to help us create the systems we so desperately needed. Equally important to the coaching was the support we received. For the first time since I planted a church, I felt like I wasn't alone. I now had the support, care, and insight I desperately needed.

ROB SHEPHERD

With ChurchBOOM's coaching, our church was able to create systems to fulfill the vision God gave us. We saw staff become aligned, and the conflict went away. We saw growth happen both numerically and spiritually. Under ChurchBOOM's coaching, we went from 150 in attendance to over 500.

Chris often says, "Professionals learn from coaching, amateurs learn by trial and error. For the first year and a half of being a church planter, I was an amateur. I was learning by making mistakes." Since receiving coaching from ChurchBOOM, the mistakes and learning curve have drastically gone down.

One of my favorite things about being a part of Church-BOOM and ChurchRescue is how I've been invited in to help other pastors. I've been able to help other pastors and churches by passing on the coaching I've received from ChurchBOOM to them. It's amazing to connect with others and help them know that they are not alone.

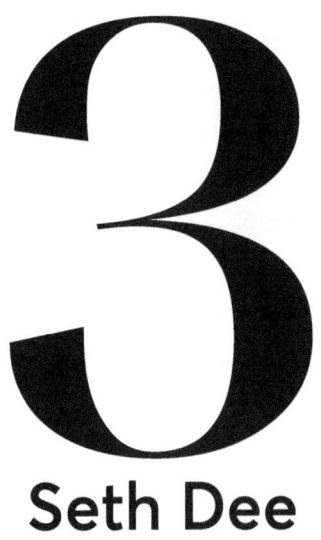

Seth Dee

I was 23 years old and the founding Pastor of our three-year-old church plant was going to move across the country. We had just gone through a difficult legal battle, where the city took from us the building we were going to purchase by eminent domain, giving us little time to find a new place to worship together. We all thought this was going to be a forever home for a church; it had everything we needed and more. It was an old YMCA building. We put a ton of work into the building and had lots of plans to see it reach its full potential. Being forced out was a huge emotional hit on the congregation and our founding pastor. We had already moved eleven times, and it was time to move again. We ended up in the local shopping mall—bringing us out of downtown where we had ministered to many people with life-controlling issues. It was a convenient spot…easy for people to walk to. Needless to say, attendance took a major hit. Now, the pastor was going to move. I was two years out of college, youth pastoring and leading worship, which had always been a dream of mine, but now things in my world were being shaken up.

I had never considered being the Senior Pastor of any church, and I quite honestly didn't have the desire. After a lot of prayer—struggling between my will and God's—He made His plan abundantly clear, so I gave my yes. I can relate a lot to Peter stepping out of the boat on stormy water; it was probably the most terrifying step of faith I've ever taken. The transition period from the time I said yes before I was thrown into full-blown leadership for this ministry was supposed to be two months, but it ended up being only two weeks. On my second Sunday at the church, we had a surprise guest speaker who I had no idea was coming, and about a week after that, my first child was born. Everything was changing fast, and I was just hanging on for dear life.

SETH DEE

Many in the church were upset about the transition, so they left with the former pastor, and many were upset but decided to stick around for a while to make my transition a whole lot of fun. On top of all these things, I was technically employed by the organization overseeing our church plant, and it had me fire several other employees within the first month of leading, the company later shut down completely because they had gotten in over their heads, taking over $300,000 from our church that was given to aid in purchasing a building with them. Now more people were angry and more people were hurting. I was experiencing some of these same feelings while trying to forgive, be humble, comfort others, and learn how to lead a church. I was completely unprepared, completely in over my head, and I felt like I was just trying to stay alive and keep breathing. Don't get me wrong—it wasn't all bad—we kept seeing God save, heal, deliver, and change people's lives. However, when it came to leadership, I didn't have the first clue about what I was doing. I had no training, no experience, and I felt pretty isolated.

I have a great love for the people of our church. It was the only reason I had to stay. I was mourning the losses like everyone else, but I had a responsibility to lead people through it all at the same time. This was the first

Reviving the Church in America

time in my life I experienced a little something called anxiety—I felt alone, I felt clueless about how to lead a church, I feared rejection from the people I loved, and I feared that my church would fail. Eventually, my family started to catch up with me. Some days it was just a pain in my chest. I had a plethora of physical medical issues come up because of the anxiety, and on other days, it literally crippled me. I often thought about throwing in the towel, but quitting was not something I was very familiar with—especially since I knew God had called me to be in the position I was in. Looking back, I probably should have called my overseers, shared my struggles, shared where I was at, and asked for help. What I did instead was bury myself in work, numb myself emotionally, and convince myself that I didn't deserve to have fun because I wasn't successful. I wasn't finding joy in ministry anymore, and prior to pastoring, I loved being in ministry. Somehow, I managed to stick it out until 2020 when God began to deal with the anxiety I was experiencing through His wise counsel in the scriptures. I don't think I could have survived the worldwide disaster without those tools, but I still had another problem—I was totally discouraged in my leadership. I had the tools to deal with the anxiety caused by my failure to thrive as a leader, but I didn't have the tools to become a better leader, and I didn't really know where to look for them. I tried leadership podcasts, and they helped, but they weren't entirely specific to my situation. I needed something a little more personal and tailored. That's where Church Rescue came into the picture. I wasn't looking for them, nor was I asking for help (and let's be clear, I should have been), but God knew what I needed, and He made the arrangement. My overseers had set up an opportunity with just five leaders from our entire organization to be part of a special leadership cohort to empower us—and boy did we need it with all the new challenges that were coming our way. Somehow, I made it onto the list of the few leaders involved, and Church Rescue was an absolute game changer for me.

> Suddenly, trying became easier because failing didn't hurt as bad; it just presented new opportunities.

I went from being completely unsure that I should be in any type of leadership position to being confident that I could grow and thrive as a leader. The practical tools that Church Rescue brought to the table for the life of the church were what helped us. It was like I had blind spots in my leadership of the church that I didn't know existed until they were shown to me by someone with a different vantage point. We had a revolving door—new people coming but never sticking around—with no process or plan to stop it. Church Rescue helped change that. We had trouble getting people to invite people to church and had no plan to get people to do it, but Church Rescue reversed that. We had toxic leaders that I was scared to deal with but Church Rescue gave me both the tools and accountability to work with them. I wasn't sure where to start when it came to leadership but with the help of my leadership coach, I began to grow, and I continue to grow and adapt to new challenges along the way. My sense of feeling alone started to depart, and I finally felt like I had plans to move forward. Confidence was the most valuable contribution Church Rescue gave to my world. It changed so much. It's really difficult to lead from a position of already feeling defeated because every hit feels like you are being kicked while you're already on the floor. Suddenly, trying became easier because failing didn't hurt as bad; it just presented new opportunities. I remember the moment it clicked that things were really changing—when other people started to acknowledge the growth in me. The other amazing thing was that I didn't take criticism so personally anymore. I was able to listen, learn from what was true, and remain unphased by the things that weren't true. There was a real sense of stability that was brought into my personal life and the life of the church through coaching, encouragement, teaching, and belief.

Prior to coaching, there were a lot of unchecked problems. As a leader without confidence, I didn't feel capable of confrontations that were long overdue and I avoided them in the name of "love", but it was the worst thing I could have done for the church and our leadership teams. Coaching gave me tools for effective communication, and I started to tackle issues head-on, in healthy ways, that brought about positive results. Our leadership structure drastically improved as teams were developed, and trust was increasing. The overall life of the church started to gain momentum again; we saw that God was working and that great things were possible. The root of so many issues within the church was a direct result of my lack of confidence… which was a direct result of the lack of tools at my disposal to lead.

I should have asked for help and searched for a coach long before I was afforded the opportunity, but I'm thankful to God that He graciously led me to Church Rescue while I was aimlessly wandering.

Tony Orlando

Nobody should ever walk alone. The journey of church planting is a paradox of sorts. It is one of recruiting a great launch team around you, with plenty of vision, coupled with energy and passion, while the leader simultaneously feels isolated and alone. It is extremely lonely at the top. After serving at a larger church, LifePoint Church in San Diego, CA, with multiple staff pastors in constant collaboration for nearly a decade, church planting has involved sitting at the local coffee shop by myself, longing for input, permission, and even help, and then suddenly looking over my shoulder and realizing that there is no one there.

Anytime you launch anything, whether a business, side hustle, or even a church, there is always the challenge of critical mass—having enough momentum, people, leadership, or clients to create a tipping point that will get you to the next level of organizational growth. As I reflect upon the early years of our church start-up, there were moments of doubt and struggle that led to discouragement and even asking the question, "Was I even called to begin with?" or "Why did I leave a nice job at a larger church for this?" I recall that chapter like it was yesterday. The low point appeared when service started. The worship team would kick off with an upbeat song as the countdown clock struck 00:00, and I, standing in the back of the room, would observe that there were more people in the band than in the crowd!!! I would go to the bathroom and wash my face, give myself the pre-sermon Rocky Balboa pep talk (while "Eye of the Tiger" was playing in my head), and somehow muster enough energy and will to deliver God's Word without anyone in the crowd knowing my internal struggle. What was wrong with me? Did I miss the voice of God?

TONY ORLANDO

My wife, who has always been a tremendous support to the ministry, constantly by my side, and there for every season and every moment, asked me the hard question, "Are you 'ALL IN'?" My current reality was that our church plant was on life support. The church could barely afford to pay me part-time, so I found myself consumed with being co-vocational, which is distracting but still part of the process of survival. With barely enough breath to expel the words, my answer was, "I'm not sure." She quickly responded with, "Well, I am… and you need to figure it out because we're in this together!!!"

The silence while I waited for the Lord to answer my questions was deafening, which led me to ask, "Why?" With no answer after months of asking, I began to shift my focus to gratitude. Instead of asking, "Why?" I began to say, "Thank you." "Thank you, Lord, for those who are here and those who are serving and giving. Thank you to those who are claiming this church as their home. Thank you for seeing something in me to plant this church. I'm not special, I'm not more talented, I'm not even qualified, but you called me. You didn't call everybody to walk this journey. Thank you for having the confidence in me to carry out this call."

Reviving the Church in America

Not long after that, I was introduced to Church Rescue. They have been there for me and our church since pre-COVID to help me navigate cultural issues and power struggles, as well as gain clarity and focus. Then, fast forward to the post-pandemic culture that we find ourselves in currently, and they have continued to stand in our corner as a coach, mentor, and silent partner. They have always offered the most practical advice—not cookie cutter—but tailor-made to fit our church and its contextual needs. It is like knowing you can call on your big brother no matter what the circumstance or how big the ask is, and they will be there. They serve unconditionally, love abundantly, and serve with great humility. Our church is better because of the help that Church Rescue has offered. We are forever grateful for the partnership that Church Rescue has given us. You are not simply friends; you are family. Thank you for your commitment to continue to see the Great Commission as not simply an option to be considered but a commandment to be obeyed.

Dan Zemlicka

My name is Dan Zemlicka, the pastor of Clovis First Assembly of God, on the corner of Sunnyside and Barstow in Fresno, California. We are a small congregation with forty-two active members and less than seventy-five regular attendees.

I have participated in the Church Boom-sponsored Coaching Network and Cohorts every month. Also, Chris Sonksen has come to speak at our church in the past. He has given us some excellent thoughts and insights that our church has implemented. We have put many of them into practice and have yielded results. We have worked on creating a more welcoming atmosphere when people come onto our church campus on Sunday mornings and have added more greeters. Many are greeting people who are coming in from the parking lot, and many are greeting people at the entrance of the church.

My first thought in sharing the struggles that we've experienced in ministry is well-stated in the following verse:

"For our struggle is not against flesh and blood, but against the rulers, against the authorities, against the powers of this dark world and against the spiritual forces of evil in the heavenly realms" (Ephesians 6:12, NIV).

Our greatest enemy to the church is indeed spiritual, and it is "in the heavenly realms," or as the NKJV reads, *"heavenly places."* Certainly, that is a fact for every church, ministry, and organization that is truly dedicated to bringing glory to God. However, here in Clovis, I need to mention that we have had some rather hard struggles in the physical places too—especially since we are a small church in an old building. The building that is our sanctuary was moved here from another property in Fresno, CA in the mid-1960s. It was the only building on the property until 1998. We purchased a portable nineteen-by-thirty-eight-foot building from a local business and installed it on the property to be used as a youth/children's building. In 2007-2008, we started working on plans to add a couple more portable buildings to accommodate the expansion of growth. We were required to make these buildings look similar to the buildings already on the property. So, we agreed and set up a twenty-four by sixty-foot building and a twenty-four by forty-foot building.

I must admit that the root of some of the "physical" problems we experience is ultimately because of those *spiritual forces of evil*; nevertheless, there have been many physical situations for which we have been hard-pressed that really didn't feel very "spiritual."

In my thirty years as pastor of Clovis First Assembly of God, I've seen a lot. For instance, we had worked through a time when we were financially strapped, and the roof of the church sanctuary needed to be replaced. One of the local churches found out about what our church was facing, and we received an offering to help us re-roof the church. We have had several miracle blessings like that, and we are truly grateful to God. In another instance, we needed more storage for different tools and maintenance supplies. Miraculously, a person from another church purchased a twenty-foot-long steel storage container to relieve some of our storage issues.

Ministry is difficult and it takes a team of people to bring things together to work. No matter how small a church is, a team needs to be developed to help with the work of the ministry. Many people feel they have little to offer due to their limited understanding. Helping people realize they have different giftings helps to encourage them to try it for a season. I have revisited many of them in their ministries, and many times, they expressed enjoying it and found that they could do the work they were called to do.

Pressing on in the power and encouragement of the Holy Spirit is the key "Because you know that the testing of your faith produces perseverance" (James 1:3, NIV).

Maybe you thought you'd never stoop to clean a toilet, fix a broken window, or repair other things that crop up through the week. I don't believe that even the most successful pastors actually sit in their offices studying their Bible to prepare a sermon as much as they would prefer.

"But you—keep your eye on what you're doing; accept the hard times along with the good; keep the

DAN ZEMLICKA

Message alive; do a thorough job as God's servant" (2 Timothy 4:5, MSG).

Although our facility is clean and practical, the furnishing and equipment are far from state of the art. We still must try to preach the Word of God zealously.

We rejoice in seeing numerous individuals turn to Christ and be baptized in our simple sanctuary. These include individuals who were formerly thieves, drug addicts, alcoholics, people who are without, widows, and those who feel hopeless. The ministry is a community ministry set out to touch lives for the gospel as best as we can. It could be through an encouraging word for those who come to receive groceries as we pray for them about their situation before they leave with groceries. It could have been having a drive-through grocery giveaway during the pandemic. Whatever the situation, we can be who God has called us to be, and we can do what God has called us to do in our communities.

The people of Clovis First Assembly of God do indeed have heart. This is the crux of the matter in any church. When a stranger visits us, we must welcome them and do whatever makes them feel at home and comfortable. I cannot overly emphasize the need for this response.

Reviving the Church in America

I've heard too many people tell of their experience of being rudely ignored as a first-time visitor to a church. We must strive to model ourselves after Job's decree, "I was a father to the needy; I took up the case of the stranger" (Job 29:16, NIV).

Due to the pandemic, our regular church attendance numbers rapidly diminished. Like other churches, we were tightly stretched to keep functioning. We learned to provide online worship through Facebook and YouTube along with thousands of other churches. This was a big step for us in the world of technology but we were able to do it by the Grace of God. Unfortunately, having no previous experience, we soon noticed that we didn't come across with much professionalism, particularly with our music and sound. We are in the process of correcting some of these problems by changing our online format presentation.

As a pastor, in an attempt to keep up with the changing times, I want to be flexible in doing what is best for our church. But not everyone likes change, and many resist it. Frankly, because our congregation is made up of around sixty-five+ or so as the average attendee age, I often find resistance in some individuals who are quite set in their ways, particularly those who prefer the past—and like to live in the past (as you will probably find in every congregation).

Again, we try to remember what we are really fighting against. Furthermore, we recognize we cannot please all people all the time! "On the contrary, we speak as those approved by God to be entrusted with the gospel. We are not trying to please people but God, who tests our hearts" (1 Thessalonians 2:4, NIV).

Another struggle that we have encountered is our seemingly unsuccessful attempts to encourage parents with young children to remain with us. I see that so much attention is given to the youth in the majority of other churches (rightfully so since the future depends on our young ones), yet it seems that our ministry most strongly caters to older individuals and retirees (who also need attention). Regardless, it is disappointing that we haven't been able to grow in children, and of course, we have seen our elderly numbers diminishing each year.

Keeping priorities straight has been a big subject for me since I began ministry thirty years ago. I think that pastors everywhere can relate to that—there are many demands and so many needs: sermon preparations, hospital visits, new guest contact, Bible study classes,

Reviving the Church in America

counseling, new member classes, weddings, funerals, event planning, missionary response, baptisms, conferences, phone calls, board meetings, prayer, etc. I am again and again reminded of the verse, "But seek first his kingdom and his righteousness, and all these things will be given to you as well" (Matthew 6:33, NIV).

Fellowship with other pastors, mentoring, and the many great leaders in ministry throughout the world have been tremendously helpful in my struggle as God's minister. Help is out there for you, too. I so appreciate the coaching networks and cohorts of Church Boom. It has been a blessing to have a Zoom call once a month or sometimes a personal phone call with a cohort leader to discuss ideas and strategies. Having a group of local pastors to go to and share what is on your heart regularly is a great benefit, too. The help and encouragement we receive from Chris' weekly podcasts and the Zoom calls with other people who are available to resource us as a church have been a blessing, too. Understanding where we are culturally is important. It is also important to understand how we, as pastors and as the church, can reach those in the community who are struggling through whatever means. Our church has used numerous resources such as books, sermon series, and Google and internet resources that have opened up amazing avenues to assist us in our mission to proclaim the truth. And how very different it was for those who prepared the way before us—without computers and copy machines!

Admittedly, we must endure many uncomfortable situations and struggles for which we never find resolution or answers but we pray and ask God continually for His ongoing help.

When we walk with the Lord in the light of His Word, what a glory He sheds on our way! While we do His good will, He abides with us still, and with all who will trust and obey. Trust and obey, for there's no other way to be happy in Jesus, but to trust and obey.

We don't have all the answers to the "whys" of our struggles; nevertheless, for those who minister and love God, there is no alternative but to <u>trust and obey</u> in faith, because God has said, "As the heavens are higher than the earth, so are my ways higher than your ways and my thoughts than your thoughts" (Isaiah 55:9, NIV).

"Jesus replied, 'Truly I tell you, if you have faith and do not doubt, not only can you do what was done to the fig tree, but also you can say to this mountain, Go,

Reviving the Church in America

throw yourself into the sea,' and it will be done" (Matthew 21:21, NIV).

> *"Fellowship in the body of Christ is based on our allegiance to Christ. He is our standard. We may have different preferences of music, worship.... This is why God tells us in Ephesians 4:3 that we are to 'preserve the unity' within the body of Christ."*[7]

---

[7] Tony Evans, *Winning Your Spiritual Battles* (Harvest House Publishers, 2019).

Alex Lara

When I think about what Church Boom has done for our church and many others around the world, I can't help but think about the movie *Here Comes the Boom*. Kevin James plays Scott Voss, a high school teacher at a high school that was struggling so badly to stay open that they had to cut the music department due to lack of funding. Scott Voss saves the music department by becoming a mixed martial arts fighter, and he fights for the money to fund the school. Its title is symbolic of the fight Voss brought to the octagon to save that high school from closing.

Reviving the Church in America

While Church Boom is not a bunch of former pastors turned MMA fighters fighting in the UFC to raise money, they do bring the boom for the body of Christ and its local churches, not just so they can survive but also thrive. My name is Alejandro Lara, I'm the lead Pastor of Elevate Ministries in San Antonio, Texas, and I want to tell you my personal story of how Church Boom brought the boom to my life and the church I lead through their cohorts and personal coaching, as well as the community I gained just by association.

Cohorts gave me the blessing of the "know-how". I've always had the "want to"—meaning, I wanted to see my church succeed; I wanted the leadership to grow but I didn't know how to do it. For example, I've always been passionate about long-distance running and because of that, I've always been able to keep my bad late-night taco eating habits and still manage to lose weight or maintain a healthy weight. However, once I got into my thirties, it seemed like my metabolism just slammed the brakes. In other words, no matter how much I ran, my weight just kept climbing along with certain biomarkers, like my blood pressure. I wanted to be at a healthy weight again, but I just didn't know how to. Finally, I realized I needed to try something new, so I enlisted the help of a personal coach who was a two-time natural Mr. Universe who was certified in fitness and nutrition—but most importantly—had a fifteen-year track record of success with his clients. I was put in his small group workouts and immediately started gaining the "know-how" from the coach and my teammates who were further down the road in their health journey. His coaching made me realize I was doing too much cardio, not lifting enough weights, and under-fueling my body, especially in the area of protein. As soon as I began to apply what I was gleaning from my coach and teammates, the weight began to drop off. Three years later, I'm now down thirty pounds, and the weight has stayed off. Church Boom's cohorts did for me in the area of church and leadership growth what my personal fitness coach and his small workout group did for my health. Like my metabolism, our church's metabolism had plateaued at the six-year mark; our attendance wasn't growing, volunteerism was down, and finances were low. Then the global pandemic hit the entire world and that was like throwing rocket fuel on the flames of our already declining church. During the pandemic, some of our ministries were wiped out—they either left our church or no longer wanted to serve. By the time we resumed in-person services, our attendance had dwindled to thirty to forty people. We hadn't had baptisms in almost a year, our discipleship growth track was pretty much non-existent, and we had

Reviving the Church in America

no follow-up ministry in place. About a year and a half later, we were still in decline and everything I was trying wasn't working. I knew I needed to try something new, so I began to research organizations or coaches who had a proven track record in helping churches get unstuck and back on the path of growth. A pastor friend of mine, who didn't know what I was looking for, invited me to a church growth seminar that pastor Chris Sonksen was teaching and I was inspired and amazed by the testimonies of other church leaders they had helped and how pragmatic their solutions were. So immediately after the session was over, I signed up for their cohorts that center around pastor Sonksen's book *When Your Church Feels Stuck*[8] and started my cohort journey in January of 2022. Within the first couple of months, I began to gain the skills from my cohort that I had been lacking while shedding the unhealthy methods and mindsets that had been holding our church and me back as a leader. By the time December 2022 came around, we had recalibrated our mission statement and had devised a new strategy on how to bring constant awareness and carry it out. We also got very clear on our values and established them. We created a first-time guest ministry that saw forty-seven people graduate from our new members' class, re-established our discipleship program that had sixty-nine graduates, baptized

---
8 Chris Sonksen, *When Your Church Feels Stuck* (Baker Books, 2017).

forty people, and grew from sixty (on a good Sunday) to 158 on an average Sunday. Just like my personal fitness coach helped me put the pedal to the metal again when my metabolism hit the brakes, Church Boom cohorts helped our church get unstuck.

During my second year with Church Boom, I decided to take my mentoring to a deeper level by signing up for their personal coaching. I figured that if I was getting such good results at the cohort level, I could only imagine the effects it would have on our church at the personal coaching level.

Now let me backtrack a little. During my first year with Church Boom, I was doing cohorts with the Boom while taking personal coaching with another organization simultaneously. However, I quickly realized the personal coaching I was receiving was not very personalized to my situation. I liken that coaching experience to the suit I wore at my elementary graduation. It was a hand-me-down suit that was unfit for my body. The sleeves and pant length were too long; I looked like a little kid wearing his big brother's suit. We didn't have enough money to get it fitted so I had to wear the suit as is. That suit was for somebody, just not me. Likewise, the personal coaching I received from the other organization was for some leader—it was just unfit for the local church body I was leading and the needs we had. I needed something more pragmatic, hands-on, and customized. So, in my second year, I discontinued my coaching with the other organization and signed up for personal coaching with Boom. As I'm writing this, I'm six months into my coaching journey. Let me start by saying I feel like I'm wearing a custom-fitted suit now. Like a skilled seamstress who measures your body before they tailor the suit to your body type, their coaches will measure you up by doing an extensive assessment of where you are at—attendance-wise, financially, spiritually, your growth track process, your leadership capacity, etc.—before they even meet with you. Based on your weaknesses and strengths, they create a plan that is personalized to your situation. Some of the results I have seen six months into my personal coaching is our small groups participation—from 10 percent to 65 percent in our congregation. In addition, they have taught me how to do things I have never done before, like create a plan to strategically launch a second service to accommodate the growth we had been experiencing on Easter and create a second plan that we executed after we launched the second service to sustain and create momentum. Since then, the average attendance has gone from 150 to 213. Furthermore, my coach brought awareness to some of our ministerial operational blind spots and helped me take action in repurposing those ministries to be more efficient.

> I'm glad that I had people like Church Boom who go above and beyond basic coaching and actually care for the people they are called to serve and empower.

Beyond the methods, strategies, and principles they teach you, they really care for the people they coach. For example, at the start of my second year with Church Boom, my wife and I found out our 1-year-old daughter, Marianna Luz, was going to need spinal surgery on a spinal deformity she was born with. Due to the invasive nature of the surgery, my daughter was going to have to be bed-bound for a minimum of one week at the hospital after the surgery was complete. When the surgeon made me aware of what needed to happen, I was shattered, angry, and frustrated, but thank God for my coach. When I told my coach about the situation, he switched really quickly from coach to prayer warrior/counselor/someone I could just confide in and vent to. Since then, I'm happy to say the doctors have changed their mind about her needing the surgery. They went from "let's wait" to "maybe not." Nevertheless, I'm glad that I had people like Church Boom who go above and beyond basic coaching and actually care for the people they are called to serve and empower. If you're a pastor looking for personal coaching that is actually tailored to your leadership situation, then the Church Boom team are your people.

There was an unexpected blessing of making new friends that came out of my journey with Church Boom. I didn't just get content and coaching. I gained a genuine community. I felt like Solomon in 2 Chronicles 1:11-12 when he asked God for wisdom to lead the nation of Israel and God gave him that, but He also gave something he didn't even ask for, which was earthly riches and influence. Likewise, I was seeking wisdom on how to become a more skillful pastor, and God was giving it to me through my brothers, but He also gave me something I didn't ask for or expect—the riches of friendships. During my first year in the cohort, one of the brothers invited me and another cohort brother to a rest and recovery trip for pastors in Baja, Mexico for free. I couldn't believe it. While there, I was able to fellowship with pastors from all around the US. We also took some time to unpack and process the trauma and pain we had all experienced from being in the ministry and learned the importance of rest and recovery in the life of a pastor. Now, I'm not saying if you sign up for cohorts or coaching, you're going to get a free trip to Baja, Mexico, but what I am saying is that God will bless you in ways you weren't expecting. Maybe it will be life-long friendships, someone you can confide in when you need to vent, or someone who can provide insight into improving your ministry that the latest mega-church conference or seminary couldn't. While in Baja, things did get a little messy upon arrival. I discovered the airline had lost my travel bag with all my clothes, toiletries, etc. So, for the first couple of days, I wore the same outfit, but on the third day, I received some great news from the airline. They told me I had an unlimited spending limit for clothes that I would get reimbursed for, and in addition, I would receive a check for $1,500! So after buying a fur coat and some new Jordans (just playing about the fur coat, but I did buy some new Jordans), I continued to call the airline every day to check on the status of my bag. On the last day of my trip, I had given up all hope of ever seeing my travel bag; in fact, I was already at the airport in Mexico ready to come back to

Reviving the Church in America

the States. While at the airport, the airline called me—they had found my bag. Long story short, I got my bag back a few hours before I returned home. I arrived in the one-hundred-degree-plus weather of San Antonio, TX with my bag that had been lost but was restored... and with some cool items I didn't have before. For me, what I've gained from the Church Boom cohort and coaching is a lot like that trip; the hope, zeal, and passion for ministry that I had lost returned, and I also gained some blessings that I didn't have prior to Church Boom—certain skills, friendships, and confidants in Christ. Likewise, if you start this journey with Church Boom, I believe there are some things that God will restore that maybe you've lost—perhaps passion or hope for your church's future—but you will also gain some things that you never had before such as new skills, friends, and a new outlook on ministry.

Back to the movie *Here Comes the Boom*—there is one super important factor I didn't mention earlier. Scott Voss won the $50,000 prize money in the UFC! That did not happen by accident, nor did he teach himself how to fight MMA. He enlisted the help of a coach named Niko who had a proven track record of success in fighting and coaching. In the same way, my victories didn't happen by accident; they happened because I enlisted the help of Church Boom, an organization with a proven track of helping others. So, if you're a pastor looking to improve as a leader and are seeking some wins for your church, it won't happen by accident. I encourage you to sign up for their coaching or cohorts today.

Vinny Greene

Our story with Church Rescue began in late 2018. My pregnant wife, two kids, and I left a wonderful church in Maine where we were assistant pastors to pursue God's calling on our lives in Vermont! I know what you might be thinking, and yes, there are more deer than people in this state, and yes, we are the home state of Bernie Sanders and Ben and Jerry's ice cream. We're also known for the fall foliage and the wonderful green mountains but one thing we are not known for in Vermont is being Christian. Vermont is infamously known for consistently topping the list as one of the least evangelized states in the country. Vermont made the state of Maine feel like the Bible Belt and we knew we were in for an immense challenge, but that is what God called us to, and He put a mission in our hearts to reach those far from God and help people walk in the fullness and power of Jesus Christ in everyday life! What better place to do that than a place where there were almost no Christians? The only problem was that we had a vision and lots of passion but no idea how to make it happen.

An interesting start:

Our first Sunday as the new pastors of Roadside Chapel in Rutland Vermont was awesome. I remember waking up that Sunday morning ready for God to do something absolutely amazing! I wasn't expecting hundreds of people during the first service but was surprised to see an almost empty church. Altogether, kids and adults combined, we had thirty-three people. It was a lower number than I was expecting and a much quieter atmosphere than I was used to, but there was a sense of expectation in the room. Surprisingly, I wasn't discouraged and left that Sunday feeling like God was going to start doing something great in this little church. Though there were few people, the people who were there loved God and wanted to see God move. This was not an accident and I want to give honor to the previous three pastors that came before me. They did an amazing job with the people God sent them and the church was blessed to have those men of God lead the church over the years. When I became the pastor, I was only the fourth pastor in the nearly seventy years of its existence. The pastor before me faithfully served the church and the people of this community for many years and I have a great deal of respect for the man of God that he is and the character that he has. God made it clear to me right away that my task wasn't to compare the work He was about to do with the work He had done over the years. It was going to be different. He was getting ready to do a new work, and I had the privilege of being a part of that.

With one Sunday in the books, we were off and running. Our expectations were high, and our faith was even higher. The first Sunday went so great—I had a strong feeling we would see a change in attendance the second week. Well, I was correct. We did such an amazing job the week before that, but on our second Sunday, we saw the attendance go from thirty-three to only thirty-eight. Not exactly the direction we were hoping for.

Still, I wasn't discouraged. It was only our second Sunday, and I knew we had a couple of things going for us. There was a small group of prayer warriors in the church, and the congregation, though small, was full of faith, believing God to do great things, and the Lord had given me a vision for Rutland. I knew where we were going; I just didn't know how we were going to get there.

It was also at this time the Lord reminded me of what God spoke to the minor prophet Zechariah:

"Do not despise these small beginnings, for the Lord rejoices to see the work begin, to see the plumb line in Zerubbabel's hand" (Zechariah 4:10, NLT).

DISCOURAGEMENT

Over the next year, we saw some steady growth, and the attendance was gradually increasing. People were getting saved and we started to see a couple of families with children start attending. There was definitely a sense of optimism in the church.

While all that was happening, I was struggling internally because all I could see was the landmines that lay ahead. I was working a minimum of ninety hours per week and doing absolutely everything that I could do to make this thing grow. Though we were growing slightly, there didn't seem to be anything "sticky" about the church for certain demographics. What I observed was that most first-time visitors who were either unchurched, young families, or people under the age of fifty wouldn't come back. It was challenging because I would never get any good feedback from any of the visitors as to why they didn't come back. They would all say, "It was great, and who knows, maybe you'll see us again sometime." I hated hearing that because I soon learned that meant they were never coming back again.

There was one couple who visited who had a different response, and I'm very thankful for it. They left their information on a connection card, and it said, "Looking forward to chatting." When I called, they started to share about all the wrong things they observed. I immediately thought to myself, "Okay, here we go." But as they shared, I realized they were simply pointing out the things I had noticed and was wanting to change. This was turning into an opportunity to get some real feedback even though I had a feeling it was going to hurt, a lot. They said it was a very confusing place. It was both welcoming and cold at the same time. The aesthetics made them think that a pastor in his sixties, seventies, or eighties was going to get up and preach but were surprised when

Reviving the Church in America

a young pastor in his thirties got up there. They felt like the church wanted to be young and vibrant but there weren't many young people, and the church was not vibrant. They said because they had experience in ministry, they could tell what was happening: it was a church that was in the process of changing but most people wouldn't get that. They started to pinpoint the challenges we were having in getting some people to return. Out of all the things they said, this was the kicker, "You probably get a lot of people that say, 'It was great, and who knows, maybe you'll see us again sometime.' And by now you've realized they'll never be back." At that, I began to laugh very hard on the other side of the phone and simply told them that they had pretty much hit the nail on the head. I also said, "You've described to me what the problems are. Do you have any suggested solutions?" Their response was, "Well, you really have two options. First, go somewhere else where the culture fits your style of ministry or talk to someone who can help you make it happen here."

God had called us to Vermont, so I knew the first option wasn't an option. I didn't even consider it. I was determined to see God do something amazing at this little church in the state of Vermont, but I knew something needed to change. The famous leadership guru John

VINNY GREENE

Maxwell once said, "If I wanted to make a difference ... wishing for things to change wouldn't make them change. Hoping for improvements wouldn't bring them. Dreaming wouldn't provide all the answers I needed. Vision wouldn't be enough to bring transformation to me or others."[9]

What I needed was a coach, mentor, or just someone to help me take everything I've read in books about church growth and put it into practice in a practical way. I began to make phone calls and made inquiries with people I thought might be able to help. I quickly learned that there weren't too many people jumping at the chance to help a church in the middle of Vermont that was only running one hundred or so people. So, I began to pray, and while I waited for an answer to that prayer, I decided to work hard and invest in as many people as I could. Toward the end of 2019, the church continued to gain momentum slowly and steadily. People were coming to know Jesus, and our kids' church was growing. I was still very aware of the holes in the ministry that needed to be fixed but at least we were heading in the right direction. We were excited for 2020 because we just knew this was going to be a year to break through some barriers and nothing could stop it ... or so I thought.

---

9   John C. Maxwell, Intentional Living: Choosing a Life That Matters

Help was on the way but not in the way that I thought.

> Little did I know this was going to turn out to be one of the most pivotal partnerships I could ever have made, and it came at just the right time.

The new year came and right away, I began to see an answer to prayer. I got an email inviting me to join a coaching Zoom call that was geared toward helping churches break 200. It was through an organization named Church Boom, and they were doing it for free. Free doesn't always equal quality, but I was desperate and willing to try anything. Little did I know this was going to turn out to be one of the most pivotal partnerships I could ever have made, and it came at just the right time. See, 2020 didn't just come with opportunities. It also came with a "small" situation called a pandemic. Churches were already closing at a rapid pace in the United States before COVID-19, but the pandemic resulted in thousands of churches closing their doors permanently.

VINNY GREENE

In March 2020, I had my first coaching call with Church Rescue (the very first one they did, I believe). At this point, our church's attendance was between 110-120 on average, and we would frequently see it drop to eighty or ninety. Right from the first session, I knew I had struck gold. Each month, we had a coaching session and were given homework. It was a step-by-step training process that made church growth more achievable. Because of the hands-on nature of the coaching, I was able to grow in my personal leadership and how I worked with people. It's one thing to know a lot about leadership and a very different thing to know how to lead. The sessions were not just a set of cookie-cutter systems to plug and play but a guide to growing the church and the pastor. I believe this was huge in helping the church grow into a healthy one. There was a strategy to going from a personality-driven growth—which my personality could only take me so far, if you know what I mean—to a process-driven approach. Even though there was a pandemic happening, and the way we did church had to look different and be done differently, the principles I learned worked regardless of outside circumstances. Church Rescue was able to walk alongside us and help us integrate new concepts and ideas that had never been done at our church before. A pivotal moment for us was when we moved from doing drive-in church to in-person church again. People who never attended church before the pandemic started to attend our drive-in church services. How were we going to get them from the parking lot to the "pew", so to speak? The great thing about Church Rescue's approach was that I was able to get real-time coaching on how to solve that problem. I got an action plan, put the principles into action, and we went for it. We opened with two services to give people room and though we didn't break any attendance records, people showed up! It was after that Sunday that I was reminded of something I once heard, "If we take care of the people God sends us, He will send us more." With everything we were learning through Church Rescue, we were equipped to take care of all that God would send us, and I had a feeling His plan wasn't to simply fill the building once but to fill it twice. I knew from that first Sunday back we were probably never going back to one service.

After about six months into the Church Rescue coaching, we broke 150 for the first time. Depending on your context, that might not sound significant, but 150 was more than anything the church had ever seen pre-pandemic. I also want to remind you that we are in a state with an average church attendance of thirty-five. Only two-and-a-half percent of the entire population goes to church anywhere, so 150 people seemed like an amazing breakthrough. So, after an insanely challenging and crazy year, we ended 2020 averaging between 120-130 people in attendance and would frequently see 150 or so people. Now, sometimes churches can get fixated on the numbers and obsess over attendance. I share some of these numbers just as a reference point. In fact, the more coaching I got, the less I focused on the size of the church. I became more and more focused on what really mattered—growing a healthy church, not a big one. Every number is a soul and every soul matters to God. Through the help of Church Rescue, I was learning how to steward the souls the Lord was putting in the Church. I was also learning how to steward the amazing leaders who were starting to rise up and help with the mission.

The next year, we continued to see an increase—an increase in attendance, salvations, baptisms, and volunteering. Our church now had an "invite culture", and people were not only visiting but staying. In 2021, we broke the 200 barrier, but more importantly, we were seeing a healthy community. Even though the official coaching was over, I was able to stay in contact with Church Boom, and they continue to be there to help. In 2022, we broke through 250 and as of the time of this

Reviving the Church in America

writing, in 2023, we've had over 300 people in attendance multiple times this year. In the past four weeks, we've had twenty-four salvations and twelve baptisms. Why am I sharing all these numbers? I know it could easily come across as bragging or prideful but here's what you need to know: I'm in an almost completely unknown place. I'm a pastor, just like thousands of other pastors who don't have a big name and don't desire a big name. We just want to be faithful to what God gave us and steward it well. We want to bring glory to God, bring as many people into the Kingdom of God as possible, and equip others to do the same. I share this with you because if God can do this through a pastor like me, in a place like this, then He can do it anywhere and with anyone willing and teachable.

In his book, *When Your Church Feels Stuck*, Chris Sonksen said, "God determines the talent, but we determine the choices."[10] So many of us might think our biggest limitation is the amount of talent we have but I've realized that the bigger hindrance is choosing not to connect with and learn from those who can help us. I believe we have all the talent we need to complete the assignment God has given us—we just need the right coaching.

---
10 Chris Sonksen, *When Your Church Feels Stuck: 7 Unavoidable Questions Every Leader Must Answer* (Baker Books, 2017).

Dan Edwards

It's an honor to tell my story, and I'm hoping it will encourage many other pastors and church planters to feel like they are not alone in their struggles. I love reading these books about people who are approachable and offer practical steps to take. Sometimes we just need to share our stories and reach out to someone we can trust. Remember, if you ever find yourself struggling to overcome anything, here is how we overcome. It's by the blood of the Lamb and the word of our testimony. I hope you find us worthy of your trust. Here is a little bit about my story. My name is Dan Edwards, and I am currently residing in Groveport, OH.

I didn't really grow up in church as a kid or teenager. I went to some youth group things but here is where things got real. As a senior in high school, I was using a basketball scholarship to get as far away from my house in Mississippi as possible. I ended up getting a full-ride scholarship to a Bible college, of all places. I think God knew the right carrot to dangle in front of me. I took the bait easily, but things changed as soon as I got on campus. I signed up for English, math, science, and prerequisite courses. After all, I was using the Bible college to transfer divisions one year later. I wanted to red-shirt and just do my thing. God had His plans, though. On the very first day of chapel, I looked around at all the Christians and thought to myself, *I never want to be like them. I never want to try and impress someone with my prayers or with how high my hands are raised.* It just looked like a show to me. I said, "God, I never want to have the mic in my hands if this is what it's all about. The lead pastor then came barging through the chapel doors and said, "I'm sorry, but we are going back to being the school of the spirit." If you want a refund or have an issue, take it up with admissions and they are happy to settle all accounts. Well, the pastor just canceled every class I had. While sorting out my files, they asked if I could sing. My polite answer was no. They asked me if I wanted to travel the world somewhere and preach the gospel. I couldn't even fathom what they were asking so, again, it was a no. They asked me if I could handle church leadership and be in a generalized class. I didn't want to be "generally" doing anything; I wanted to do something important and something that would last. I asked where my file was placed, and they said "pastoral." I said, "Just leave it there." That's how I started my walk with God. I eventually repented in my dorm room and finally understood his call on my life, but it took a while.

After Bible college, I started in youth ministry. I loved every second of the front lines in youth ministry. I spent nine years pouring into kids and watching them grow up and become worship leaders, youth leaders, and dedicated, productive, and engaged leaders in their churches. I was just a volunteer youth pastor at first. I climbed the ranks and went to being a part-time paid employee and then looked out of state for a full-time opportunity.

I moved to a Marine Corps community in Jacksonville, NC. These men were men. I loved serving alongside my church as a youth pastor but boy was it hard. My pastor ate breakfast with President Bush and was in charge of

Reviving the Church in America

Helicopter Fleet 1 while he was serving at the very top of the leadership chain. My pastor taught me so much about structure, but it wasn't easy at all. He was training me the only way he knew how. The Marine Corps way. I think it would help every young man to serve a couple of years in a military capacity but I told my pastor I signed up for the ministry, not the military. We had a good laugh, and I learned a lot about obedience and disobedience. I really feel that my task was to learn while I was there. We had a thriving youth group that quadrupled. In all of the hard moments, the kids always kept me there. I knew I had a job to do, and I needed to do it until it was finished.

Things were great. My house was my home and I loved where I lived at the time. Everything was going well and I was very comfortable. Then, suddenly things changed. The house where I was so happy at now felt like I was living out of a hotel room. I felt like I was living in a makeshift scenario and all I wanted to do was find my home again. I knew it was out there somewhere and I couldn't wait to find my calling, my ministry, and feel at home again. My heart changed in an instant. I felt my heart click and turn. My pastor confirmed I was ready. Just like that, I was no longer in youth ministry but found myself church-planting. I moved to Mississippi (of all places) and took over a dilapidated building. I even found two couples to eventually help me launch the church. My beautiful wife, Amanda, and I were doing everything we could do to get this church plant going. Our motto was "make it happen". We had the support of our state leadership and things were going great. We even grew the church the old-fashioned way and had our son Noah, who joined Ella and Ethan. Our family of five really started to make a difference in our community. We were humble, hungry, and hustling! Then it happened again. . . . my heart clicked and I knew this chapter was over after four years. My church was solid and in good hands. I always realized it was God's church, and I knew he would take care of His church—after all—it's His bride.

Now what? I thought God was going to do something amazing and the red carpet would be rolled out as I headed back to our home state in Ohio. Boy was I wrong, I couldn't even volunteer as a pastor for free. I had a church tell me that. What was God doing and why was this so hard? I knew I was called to come back to Ohio, but nothing was working out. I had family troubles, work troubles, and no leads for a new ministry position. I know what you're thinking, *who quits a good job, in a good situation, and doesn't have a plan?* I didn't even have a place to go. All I had was obedience, and that was enough. Read that again, all I had was obedience, and that was enough!

I was working in a body shop on old classic cars, restoring them to their former beauty, when my father-in-law said, "I know a friend who has been wanting to retire and needs help turning his church over to a young couple. We were thrilled to have breakfast the next day with this pastor. It turns out we were the answer to his prayers. We immediately got to work with his ten congregants. I know what you're thinking ... *great job guy, you left your good church for ten people and a pastor who wants to retire.* Yeah. It actually got worse—much worse.

I took these ten faithful people who had served with this pastor for twenty-nine years, and I asked them to do the most audacious thing ever. I asked them to change. That's when I knew this wasn't going to be easy. Cue the rocky music and enter the ring. I fought a good fight; I got those ten people out of a homeless shelter's chapel and into a new industrial office space. It only took a homeless lady pushing and pulling a knife on my wife to make that change occur. I thought, *How hard could this be?* We took ten people and grew to thirty-five, and we even found a church renting the space after us with thirty people and no pastor. They joined us for Easter, and BOOM, just like that, we doubled and acquired them over a couple of months.

Things couldn't have been better . . . until COVID hit. I couldn't see how unhealthy my leadership style and lack of systems were until everything came screeching to a halt during the pandemic. I came to realize I was not really pastoring. The retired pastor (yeah, I forgot to mention he didn't retire) and I were such a good team, and I didn't want to do ministry alone, so we tag-teamed things. I was ultimately just being disobedient but was scared and lacked self-confidence. I realized I leaned on him too much, and as our building lease expired, we went our separate ways. He went into a blaze of glory with grandkids, and I remained to fight the fight alone. We are still good friends to this day, and I admire all he did for me. If only I could be that cool in my late sixties.

It didn't take long to realize what a great man he was and how much I missed him. I went right into another small church acquisition. I mean, we didn't have a building and this church in Groveport, OH didn't have a pastor. It happened to be where I first started youth pastoring! Here we go. . . . I thought it was going to be easy. We had three churches' building funds stashed away, we had sixty+ people, and these are all the faithful people from small churches holding on in dire situations. This was all going to come full circle, right?

It didn't take long to figure out why each church had failed, and I could see now that the failing mindsets were still in the people. Change is hard for folks, and I began preaching, teaching, training, and so on over and over again, and no one really wanted to change. Then I saw the light. The Church Boom Roundtable email popped up and only one person would go with me. It was the kid's director. She said, "Wow, this was better than any seminar I have ever attended." I quickly seconded that comment. As we were talking, this man shook my hand, put his arm around me, and just started talking to me. I quickly recognized him as Chris Sonksen, the main speaker. He said, "Hey, get your phone, I'm going to give you my cell phone number. I want you to call me." Okay, no way was I going to call a nationally known speaker who has a ton of books, right? I'm just me. Did he realize who I was? More importantly, who I thought I wasn't?

Well, the sad part of my story is coming up. You may want to get the tissues out! I was only thirty-six years old at that time, and I had a stroke! It had been a couple of days of weird mistakes in my speech. I was so cheap that

DAN EDWARDS

I didn't want to pay for a doctor's visit, so I tried to find a blood pressure machine at the pharmacy. Well, thanks to COVID, those were no longer available. I went to the doctor's office to see if they would check it for free, and they said yes, of course. The nurse turned white as a ghost and checked it three times. She said, "I will be right back." Immediately the doctor entered and said, "How are you feeling?" My response was, "I'm fine, I just need a pill or something." He said, "No, we need an ambulance. I'm afraid you are having a stroke." I immediately went to an emergency room at the nearby hospital. The doctor there told me my brain was bleeding! He said, "Call your wife and tell her to get here quickly. We are transferring you to another hospital." He then said, "Now call your kids and tell them you love them." I said, "Doc, come on! Really? I'm fine." He said, "No you're not; if your brain doesn't stop bleeding, you will die." Thanks for no hope, Doc! It was horrible being alone during this time. Because of COVID, this was the worst possible time for this to have happened. The ministry was defeating me. My health was defeating me. I was losing this fight and there was no way I could maintain this pace or withstand this beating. My wife and I had hours-long conversations about ministry and stress. "They say" stress will kill you. I don't know who "they" are, but they were not lying. I found myself not wanting to do ministry stuff the same way anymore, and I *really* knew I didn't want to do it alone. I needed help, coaching, or something. I needed to find someone who not only knew how to do this but wanted to do ministry with me. Very few people will actually get their hands dirty in ministry, and we all know how messy ministry can be.

Well, yours truly never called Pastor Chris Sonksen back but the Church Boom round table stuck with me. How cool was it that they were rescuing churches and coaching pastors? I got into a cohort and then as a year passed, many things changed for me. There was another roundtable. I knew if I could get as many leaders and volunteers as possible to the roundtable, then they would see a need for a coach! I had sixteen people show up!!! They were all floored as the speakers leveled us with practical solutions to all of the problems we were having as a church. My leaders also saw the need for me to seek help. They all loved me, but after the stroke, they knew things needed to change, or I wouldn't be in ministry much longer.

> Pastors, let me tell you, there is a difference between asking and saying what you need.

DAN EDWARDS

As the speakers wrapped up, none other than Pastor Chris put his arm around me. Before I could tell him how inspired I was or how I brought my whole team here to catch the vision of Church Boom, Pastor Chris said, "You never called me." I was speechless, and let me tell you, my wife will testify that's a hard thing to do for me. He repeated and said it with all sincerity, "You never called me." He remembered that from two years ago! Well, needless to say, we talked so much more, and I surely followed up by calling him several times. We connected and I asked my board if I could get some coaching. This was the second time I had asked the board that question. Pastors, let me tell you, there is a difference between asking and saying what you need. Be bold and tell your board what you need to be successful in ministry. I hadn't told them with enough conviction in the past, but this time, I made a case for why this would help me and ultimately, the church. They agreed this time because they saw the need after attending the roundtable. I called Pastor Chris and said, "We are now ready for a coach. I got approval from the board, and we also want to rescue a church with a generous donation." Pastor Chris replied, "I will take you on and coach you guys."

Reviving the Church in America

We have never looked back, the more our people receive training and coaching from Church Boom speakers, the more we have grown. We started to implement healthy systems, and everyone could see a clear picture of our ministry. For once, we could all look at the same picture. I tried to cast my vision, but it was never clear. I tried on my own until I was blue in the face. It took another voice for people to hear the need that I was trying to convey. It didn't take long before I felt we had a team atmosphere. People were ministering and volunteering, knowing that the church would now grow. Not only that, but I no longer felt alone. I had someone coaching me and loving me. I realized that now that I had a coach and a game plan, all I needed to do was execute. The execution is my responsibility. Church Boom could give me all the resources I needed for growth, but I had to implement those strategies and systems.

Church Boom took me from a church that needed rescue to a church that is now rescuing other churches in need. I am part of a team, and I'm doing ministry together with other great leaders. If you find yourself in need of coaching, resources, pastoral friends, systems, and encouragement, then you have found yourself reading the right book. I pray God works on your heart and leads you to consider the Church Boom resources.

DAN EDWARDS

Ask questions and find the answers you have been looking for like I did. God bless you. Don't make the same mistake as I did. Make the call to get help. It's not just the ministry that may be suffering. If you are suffering, let us help you.

If you are like me—never wanting to have the microphone in your hand but now feel God is calling you there—we are here to help you every step of the way and make sure you feel resourced and equipped to do all God has called you to do.

Bryan Hallmark

I became the pastor of Christian Life in April of 2019. I came into a church that was in a mass exodus. There were around eighty people left, and most of them were over fifty years of age. The church's bank account was negative, they were two months past due on the mortgage, and the third one was now due. There was no spending to begin with because there was nothing to spend. We had a team of elders who told me they run any and all events. They do the decorating and planning. I was trying to update the church and bring in new families. I knew they could not lead the way if we were going to reach the younger generation. All of our programs had a 1980s feel. The church was not reaching anyone. The methods were not there, the structures were not in place, and there sure wasn't any money to do anything with.

Easter was a week away, and I felt overwhelmed out of the gate. No one was leading anything. I was trying to figure out what to do first. There were no structures or systems in place. I felt like the boat was sinking and no one was bailing water. A young lady was overseeing the kid's church. No one knew her or her husband. He didn't attend church. They always smelled like cigarettes, and they were never on time. There were no youth ministries or young adult ministries. There was a guy on the keyboard who was singing songs from the eighties. He had a young lady singing backup vocals, and she was off-tune. The projector was dim, and the house lights were too. They had Styrofoam cups painted on a board as a backdrop on the stage. The church was going down fast. I had many conversations about the finances of the church with our network pastor and about how the church is weeks from closing its doors. I completely understood why. The church desperately needed young, strong, mature leadership. Someone had to make the necessary changes—and fast—or this church would be nothing more than a memory.

My first sermon was on Matthew 16:17-18 (NIV): "Jesus replied, 'Blessed are you, Simon son of Jonah, for this was not revealed to you by flesh and blood, but by my Father in heaven. And I tell you that you are Peter, and on this rock, I will build my church, and the gates of Hades will not overcome it.'" I knew I believed in this, but I had to instill this in the people that remained. I had to preach to myself a little that day. But when I was done, I felt like I could charge hell with a squirt gun. Sadly, the people didn't. I was their answer but they hadn't yet caught on that they were God's answer. I was very intentional with the sermon series. I spoke on the power of the church. I taught how we are God's plan A, and He doesn't have a plan B. Nothing really changed. I had to deal with people who were in leadership positions before I got there. I tried to be diplomatic, but I knew it was going to take more than a conversation. They needed leadership. Well-coached leadership.

I came in with a lot of confidence but quickly felt defeated. I was dealing with what many pastors deal with. Our honeymoon period was short-lived. Criticism quickly came. I had a team leader who was going behind my back and creating division between me and the staff. I didn't see it for a long time. We would have staff meetings and once they were over, he would inform the staff that we were going to do "this" or "that". I treated him like a son and trusted him 100 percent. I made up reasons why he couldn't do these things. I felt the distance between me and my staff but just couldn't put my finger on why. Things finally blew up while he was out of town. I discovered so many things he was doing behind my back. I planned on confronting and firing him as soon as he returned from his trip. But a board member had filled him in, and he sent a nasty resignation letter by text message to me and the board. He had the entire time do the same. Verbiage was almost copied and pasted. I was beside myself. He did this on a Friday morning, and I had to preach that Sunday. My worship pastor, as well as my children's pastor, was gone, and we were back at square one after two years.

I brought this young team with me to kick off our adventure. Two of them were my sons. Just to show you a glimpse of the adventure, my wife and I are the only ones left from the team. To be fair, I was the one God called. We started strong. I quickly discovered my vision, mission, and core values. I thought that would really take us to where we needed to be. I quickly learned that a plan sounds great until you add people. We walked through great times, heartaches, disappointment, hurt, and fear. I had to release leaders and board members due to this young leader's deception and manipulation. My youngest son left for the Air Force. My oldest son and his wife stuck it out for almost four years. He was best friends with the young leader that split the church. He was so broken over the deception. Here we were, giving the church everything we had, and the biggest hurt came from inside the church, from the very team we brought with us to reach Santa Fe.

My oldest son was one of my rocks in ministry. He came to me in September of 2022 and said he felt called by God to move on. God had said the same thing to me about them. He took a worship pastor position in Austin, and I felt all alone. The love of my life, my wife Cindy, was right by my side, but I didn't have my son in the office anymore. We would lift each other up, and we had each other's backs. He was not only a strong friend in ministry but in life. Four years of fighting and struggling to get a church off the ground overwhelmed my heart. I was done. I felt like I had lost, and I needed to step away. I no longer felt like I could take the church where it needed to go. I lost my drive and dreaded Sundays. I lost the drive to preach, study, or pray. I felt attacked and alone. I couldn't bring unity to the body. I was tired of hearing, "Can you pray for me?" I needed someone to pray for me! I was exhausted and drained. I didn't know how to hear from God anymore. My team was gone, and I didn't see any hope. I was too prideful to share this with anyone. I felt I was on call twenty-four hours a day. There was an internal struggle of, "I'm the last line of defense". I didn't know how to apply a Sabbath, and I needed rest. The Word of God was not comforting me, and I felt like God had abandoned me. I felt isolated and had unrealistic expectations for my role.

I let my guard down and received counseling during this time of depression, and it was a major blessing. I felt like the emotions were finally filtered and placed in the right perspective. My therapist helped me grow emotionally, spiritually, and relationally. He gave me great self-awareness, empathy, and compassion for others. My mental health improved. I was having conflicts with my wife and would wonder why she even wanted to be with me. He helped me with my interpersonal conflicts and relationship issues. He showed me how I was carrying a huge amount of responsibility as a leader and how we are not created to do this alone. Of course, Chris Sonksen came to mind. I realized I could not do it alone anymore. I need coaches and mentors in my life to walk me through it all and help me win. My therapist taught me how to deal with spiritual concerns such as doubts, questions, and struggles with faith. I walked away from this experience realizing that I needed a coach. I needed someone who had been there and could throw me a lifeline. I'm not sure why we pastors feel we have to do this alone. That is the hardest thing in the world. We are created to do this together.

I was introduced to Chris around 2016 when Pastor Mike Dickenson, our network pastor for the Assembly of God, brought him in for a pastor's training. I never thought I needed coaching. Wasn't it for those who didn't know how to do ministry? I went years thinking I didn't need a coach. Now, I have friends that I speak to about coaching and the hardest thing to hear is, "I don't need a coach." I love what Chris always says: "Amateurs learn from mistakes; professionals get coached." Chris made a huge impact on my life at that training. I wanted to know how to put strategy to vision. I introduced myself to Chris and he volunteered his number. I was impressed but I didn't think for a minute this guy would be reachable. I remember the first time I sent him a text. He responded within five minutes. I was shocked. This guy is the real deal! I started by just asking questions. The next thing I knew, I had a coach.

Reviving the Church in America

After my son left, I hired an executive of ministries. I let him know that he must be coached. Chris made himself available. The first thing we learned was self-leadership. We had to ask ourselves the question, "Am I doing the absolute best with the talent, skill, and gift God has given us?" We took our team through the personal leadership growth worksheet. We gauged our leadership to discover where we really were. Our team had to self-reflect and discover what it really looks like to be on the other side of our leadership. It was eye-opening! Our team began to put a plan together. We started going through books together that great leaders have written. The team wrote out their leadership goals. We started listening to leadership podcasts. And everyone on the team started looking for mentors.

Next, we had to define our reality. We had to look at what was keeping our church from growing. Our team defined what church life-cycle we were in. We then identified what was right, wrong, missing, and confusing. Then we wrote out our three core action steps to take to move forward to the next stage. This led us right into discovering our mission and developing a strategy so that we could accomplish what it is that we are called to do. We knew that the culture had to change, so we developed our values, which are our guiding principles to live by. This kicked off a team campaign to increase by one hundred in a semester. We knew that to reach one hundred, we would have to measure everything we did so that we knew if we were winning are not. Chris always says, "What you don't inspect, people don't respect." All of these strategies helped us align our team. We knew whether we had the right people in the right seats. The entire church's direction began to change. This led us to change our culture from no one serving, inviting, or developing people to team recruiting and retaining, leadership ladders, and telling stories of what we want to see repeated. Now we have teams to plan better services, engage with new guests, and follow up with everyone who visits and joins teams.

> Church Rescue has not only restored life into a dying church but has developed a church that is loving and serving the community.

Our church began to see health and stability. It is not a quick six-week course, but a lifetime journey. We are recruiting and retaining leaders and volunteers like never before. People are being added to the church weekly. Small groups are taking off. People are talking about our church in the community. Our people are serving not only the body of Christ within the church but unbelievers in the community. We are meeting with city officials, serving foster care facilities, having outreaches, feeding the homeless and so much more. Church Rescue has not only restored life into a dying church but has developed a church that is loving and serving the community. We are raising up young leaders and developing them so that they can raise up those around them.

I invited Chris to come do a Rescue weekend. God placed that vision in my heart, and I have run with it. My executive is going through coaching every month and developing leaders, and leaders are developing volunteers. It has transformed our church, our people, and our community. Ministries are intentional and growing. We have surpassed our COVID numbers, and we are on the path to double our church again.

Rescue has taught me that rescued people rescue people. I am now coaching pastors and investing in them. Because Church Rescue pulled me out of the sinking sand, I now have a heart to reach out to every pastor who is sinking and pull them out. This is my second round of coaching pastors. My heart is so full when I see hope restored in pastors who are ready to quit. I am seeing their churches grow and flourish! I'm walking pastors through hurts and disappointments. The greatest thing about it all is to know that we are not alone and there are so many who care and want to walk you through whatever your church is going through. That is so empowering!

My prayer of encouragement for pastors who are feeling isolated and alone is that God has called you and others want to surround you and help you go from where you are to what God has for you. There is a family of pastors who know what you are going through, and you do not have to do it alone. No matter how dire the situation looks, God can take your church and make it healthy and strong again. You are in the right place; you just need the right people to come alongside you and help take you to where God wants you. We are better together! Ecclesiastes 4:9-12 (NIV) says:

> *Two are better than one, because they have a good return for their labor: If either of them falls down, one can help the other up. But*

Reviving the Church in America

pity anyone who falls and has no one to help them up. Also, if two lie down together, they will keep warm. But how can one keep warm alone? Though one may be overpowered, two can defend themselves. A cord of three strands is not quickly broken.

10
Charles Olmeda

"I've fallen and I can't get up!" The yell for help derives from a line in an all-too-familiar commercial advertising an emergency response and home alert system. The small device, which predominantly hangs around a person's neck, allows the individual to press a button and alert an emergency response hotline in the case of an emergency. Without it, a person with limited mobility experiencing an emergency may suffer a catastrophic loss, even death. How about you? What mechanism do you have in place to alert someone of the trouble you may be facing?

Reviving the Church in America

How about this scenario? What does a pastor with twenty-three years of experience serving the same congregation, with a post-graduate degree, serving as a professor, and engaging in a plethora of community development and consulting endeavors need from a mentor? If your answer was, "not much" or "nothing," with all due respect, you are unequivocally wrong! At first glance, the list of accomplishments may sound braggadocios. Yet, the intention serves to point out that no one is exempt from the need for guidance regardless of how small or grand their accomplishments may be. Such was the case with me and the ministry I have had the privilege of serving for twenty-three years.

HELP ME, I'M STUCK!

Chris Sonksen's book, *When Your Church Feels Stuck* succinctly captures the emotion we sensed and the pulse (at least from our perspective) of our ministry, when we became familiar with Church Boom for the first time.[11] In hindsight, knowing that God's timing is perfect, we met Chris by divine providence. The next few months would serve as a testament to God's perfect timing in what we would have initially thought was a coincidence. Our ministry was just coming out of the COVID pandemic and beginning to experience unprecedented growth. During the pandemic, God led

---
[11] Chris Sonksen, *When Your Church Feels Stuck*.

us to change the name of our church. With that came an entire re-branding of the ministry, which included a series of long overdue interior and exterior renovations. Interestingly, we unveiled the total re-branding simultaneously with the post-COVID re-opening of our church. In retrospect, it was probably one of the most counterproductive things anyone could have suggested. Yet, for us, it worked. The combination of a new name, a fresh exterior look (including a new LED sign), interior renovations, including a new café, new chairs, and a list of other upgrades, coupled with a consistent growth pattern we had not experienced in a couple of years created a need that I could not quite identify at that time—a need that, sometime later, I would categorically identity as "stuck"!

A yell for help is not indicative of failure.

Have you ever been there? At a crossroads between greatness and uncertainty? Between knowing you're on the right track but feeling like you lack the right (something) to get to the next dimension? That word

Reviving the Church in America

"something" is exactly what the emotion feels like. A sense of "What is it that I need?" or "How do I get to the next level of ministry?" If so, you're not alone. Churches and ministries of all sizes experience similar growing pains. Often, one may think that the need for growth is numerical. But growth is not limited to numbers. Sometimes our bandwidth needs to expand; that is, it must be able to handle a greater capacity of responsibility. Other times it may be our leadership, volunteers, or ministry personnel that may need growth—spiritual, academic, ministerial, or organizational. As such, the sense of being stuck is not necessarily indicative of something gone wrong. A yell for help is not indicative of failure. It may be God's way of reminding you—reminding me—that we all need people to walk alongside us and mentor us. We need people who will guide us and provide a perspective that we may not have been privy to when we suffer from doing the same thing over, and over, and over again.

Amid the proverbial crossroad, I remembered talking to a friend just a few months prior, Dr. Nick Garza, who at the time served as the Hispanic Ministry liaison for Convoy of Hope. A coincidence? Unlikely! He had mentioned that whenever I was ready to host another leadership conference, he had just the right guy to participate. I was just about to host a leadership conference open to pastors, leaders, and volunteers—from within our church and outside of our church. In short, I took Dr. Garza's recommendation and invited both to participate. Dr. Garza would serve as a keynote speaker for an opening service and Pastor Chris Sonksen would serve as a keynote speaker for a half-day of leadership workshops. Other than a few online videos of Chris (who doesn't Google, YouTube, or Vimeo the people they seek to invite?), I had never heard him speak before. However, in an instant, with a room full of leaders and emerging leaders, Chris captured the attention of the audience and framed what could have been a scripted version of where we found ourselves in ministry. We were stuck! We were sliding back and forth between good and great, between where we had been for years and where God wanted to take us. As Chris put it, we were eleven months pregnant. So, what was the problem? The problem stemmed from four key areas many ministries need to experience: a fresh voice, a renewed vision, a clear action plan, and a consistent execution of the plan.

A FRESH VOICE

In a perfect world, as pastors and leaders, we would want to believe that our voice is golden. That what we say, the wisdom we attempt to convey, and the principles we frame, become the catalysts that propel those we lead into action. Sorry to be the bearer of a rude awakening, but we are not the greatest thing since sliced bread. (Who came up with that anyway?) As a parent, I have experienced this inexplicable phenomenon time and time again—listening to your children explain how the wisdom of a stranger or the words of someone else's parent has provoked an epiphany and enlightened them to a "newfound" reality! All the while, you look at them and tell yourself, "Isn't that the very thing I have been telling them time and time again?" Relax! It's okay! I have found that when people become accustomed to hearing a voice year after year, coupled with all the nuances that come with a personal relationship, it can lead to what I call the "sin of familiarity".

Did Jesus not face the same dilemma? Can you relate to the similar voices spreading through the crevices of indifference among the people who were too familiar with Jesus's humanity that they could not perceive the unveiling of his leadership—of his anointing? Matthew 13:55-56 (NIV) puts it this way, "Isn't this the carpenter's son? Isn't his mother's name Mary, and aren't his brothers James, Joseph, Simon, and Judas? Aren't all his sisters with us? Where then did this man get all these things?" In ministry, sometimes poor treatment is not intentional, nor does it mean that people do not respect you. For some who have been in ministry for many years, particularly within the same ministry, it could mean that those closest to you have not been able to fully comprehend the "new" thing(s) God is doing in your life. I can provide you story after story of colleagues who have been involved in local church ministry for an extended period and experienced supernatural moves of God but sensed that their giftings were better received elsewhere than in their own sphere of influence. Why? Because of the sin of familiarity! Like those in Jesus's time, consequences for such actions do exist. But that is a topic for another chapter or book.

Let me recommend that you embrace the momentum that comes with a fresh voice. Do not become bitter. Allow the partnerships that God brings to you and your congregation to help you become better. In our case, Chris's voice ignited a sense of urgency. It served to help those both old and new to ministry recognize that what God was doing in their midst required "all hands on deck"! It became a clarion call to action. In full transparency, for my wife and I, it became a breath of fresh air. We had not realized that the busyness of a post-pandemic re-branded and growing ministry had us spinning in the proverbial hamster wheel of handling everyday ministry responsibilities. When that happens, we often forget that new growth requires new strategies. And if you are open to the leading of the Holy Spirit, you will realize that new strategies often come via a fresh voice—someone that God uses to help you (and your leadership) pinpoint the areas of ministry that need tweaking so that you can handle the growth that God intends to bring.

A RENEWED VISION

What happens when years of ministry responsibilities, voices clamoring for your attention, changes in personal growth, and an unexpected global pandemic intertwine to make for a perfect storm? The kind of storm that does not quite destroy you, but instead, causes enough unrest and lack of clarity to interrupt an otherwise calm day (or season)?

There is a difference between the absence of vision and a vision that has become obscured or even derailed by the unexpected—the unwelcomed challenges that tug on your leadership and cause you to focus your attention on matters that do not propel the vision forward. By vision, I do not simply mean the ability to see but to apply a framework that delineates—with clarity—where your ministry, business, or life is headed. In our case, although we understood that our calling revolved around loving people into a transformative life with Jesus Christ and making certain that everything we did glorified Him, we had lost the laser-focused attention that would help people experience that transformative experience. Our atmosphere was consistently saturated with worship, and the Word of God was preached without compromise. But where were the systems that enabled each person who encountered such powerful experiences—the first, the second, and the third-time guests—to understand the process through which they could take their experience to another level? A process that would help them engage in ministry beyond a Sunday attendance? Those processes required a renewed vision—a clear, concise, and drawn-out plan that would help revitalize the understanding of not only what God had called us to do, but how.

If someone asked you, "What is it that God has called you to do?" how would you answer that? Your answer may be "God has called me to win our neighborhood—our whole city—to Christ!" Wonderful! But "how" you will accomplish that is just as important. When God laid the burden upon Nehemiah to rebuild the walls of Jerusalem in chapters 1-3, he understood that a vision was not good enough. He needed a plan. As such, through partnerships, guidance, and a renewed vision, he understood not only what God had called him to do, but how it would be accomplished. Chris Sonksen's ability to use his pastoral experience, coupled with years of helping ministries around the country become laser-focused on executing their God-given vision, undoubtedly helped renew a vision that had been obscured by the day-to-day responsibilities of reactive behavior rather than proactive vision.

A CLEAR ACTION PLAN

"If it is going to get done with perfection, then I will have to do it myself!" Ever heard someone say that? I remember my wife saying that about our young girls and their ability (or lack thereof) to wash dishes. Although replacing them with her perfect dish-washing ability would have been ideal, it would have robbed the girls of the process of learning, growing, and perfecting. Similarly, a "how-we-are-going-to-get-there" plan of action that will help catapult a vision forward requires a clear action plan and enough people to see it through. You may say, "Pastor, those are both one and the same." No, they are not. Let me explain.

CHARLES OLMEDA

As a ministry with a clear understanding of what God had called us to do, we now understood how we needed to handle some of the things that required attention to effectively gauge the results of what we were doing. We knew that if we were going to minimize the exit of first-time guests and not lose them due to a lack of relational connections, we needed to have a system of assimilation that would increase retention. That was the how! How do you minimize the proverbial back door exit? You implement an effective assimilation strategy. That's how. However, knowing how to do something may not be enough unless you have a clear action plan. That action plan required us to engage and trust people—like our daughters at a young age—to engage in ministry opportunities. That would require a desire for perfection using imperfect people (aren't we all?)! It meant that we had to put a system in place (Chris labels this a Strategic Leadership Team), with clear, concise, and consistent instruction that would help navigate us through a process of learning, growing, and perfecting. It meant that we had to put a system in place that provided answers to, "What is being done?" "Who is doing it?" And "by when?" That is a clear action plan.

A CONSISTENT EXECUTION OF THE PLAN

The Apostle Paul wrote to the Galatians, encouraging them to "... not become weary in doing good, for at the proper time we will reap a harvest if we do not give up" (Galatians 6:9). Often, it is not the absence of a voice, a renewed vision, or a clear action plan that detracts from long-term success; it is the lack of consistency. Without giving it too much thought, I could rattle off a list of people who love new things—new programs, new ideas, and even new people. Yet, many of these same individuals cannot consistently see a program or an idea through from beginning to end with a spirit of excellence.

Nehemiah found himself in this conundrum—an abrupt halt to a clear and concise vision. Although he had a renewed vision and a clear plan, he encountered opposition in ways that discouraged his leaders and followers alike and brought his project to a screeching halt, whether he had accounted for it or not (Nehemiah 4:6-12). What will you do when discouragement sets in?

God strategically used Church Boom, via the conduit of Chris Sonksen, to serve as a timely voice and help the delivery process of that eleventh-month pregnancy. But what happens when Chris is gone? Although the relationship continues and the availability for ongoing partnership, coaching, or mentoring remains available, the truth is that long-term success requires a diligent and consistent approach to a plan. As I often tell students involved in a community mentoring program, I have the privilege of leading, and "quitting is not an option!" We cannot set plans in place and trust that they will run seamlessly and without interruption. Part of the clear plan requires consistency. Consistent monitoring! Consistent adjustments! Consistent follow-through. Consistent commitment to the renewed vision. In the process, the enemy of your soul will attempt to sabotage your progress. But as Nehemiah encouraged his leaders, let me encourage you, "... don't be afraid of them. Remember the Lord, who is great and awesome, and fight ... " (Nehemiah 4:14a). In Nehemiah's case, the wall was built to half its height when the increase in opposition rose. Did you get that? It was half its height! It had not been finished! So you, too, must remain consistent in executing the plan God has given you. Use the voices—the partnership, the coaches, or the mentors—that God has afforded you because none of us are exempt from needing people who will help us complete that task God has set before us. Remember, if you have fallen and can't get up, make sure you are proactive in putting the right mechanisms in place so that the right

Reviving the Church in America

response team—the right coaches and mentors—can help you get up and fulfill God's purpose for your life!

We are eternally grateful for the coaching and friendship of Chris Sonksen (and his team) and his willingness to serve as a behind-the-scenes catalyst to God-given visions around the country.

11

Joel Wood

In May 2016, I relocated my family to Roswell, a town of roughly 50,000 people in southeast New Mexico, to take over and revitalize a struggling church. A few years before our arrival, the church went through a significant amount of trauma under the leadership of the former pastor. They had experienced misuse of funds, moral failure by the senior pastor, and many other issues in the area of finances. To say the leader had violated this group of people would be a gross understatement. As the shock and disappointment of the failure spread through the congregation, a church that had nearly 400 in attendance weekly shrank to thirty. The result of the trauma was as expected. The church suffered. Disillusionment and hopelessness set in. The finances of the church dwindled while the needed repairs of the roughly 36,000-square-foot aging facility increased. The drywall was falling. When it rained outside, it poured inside. This was the genesis of our journey into senior leadership.

Before moving to Roswell, I launched into ministry as a youth and young adult pastor in Las Cruces, NM. I learned many valuable lessons over almost five years, but none of them would prepare me to walk into senior leadership. During our final year in Las Cruces, the Lord began to stir our hearts that a change was coming. After candidating for the lead pastor position in March 2016, my wife and I were offered the job. We were infused with hope and excitement for the future. We had the desire and drive to succeed, but we quickly learned that we needed more experience. Although blessed to be on staff at a larger church as a youth pastor, I was quickly overwhelmed by the magnitude of running a church. How was I to lead wounded people back to health, cast vision, create process, communicate with clarity, develop generosity, or define core values? How could I guide a board of elders as the youngest person in the room? How was I supposed to create a culture of generosity in a church whose finances had been severely transgressed? I had heard a story of a woman who put her wedding ring in the offering plate out of guilt. The idea of cultivating health in these areas felt out of reach!

Like many, I began the process of trial and error. Over several months, I feebly attempted to solve the issues of the church. We saw small measures of success, but many times what felt like my best idea would produce nothing. It felt like we were spinning the tires on a car—a lot of revving the engine and smoke from the tires, but we were not going anywhere. Many nights I would go home after a long day in the office to tell my wife how frustrated I was. I had a vision in my heart and no idea how to bring it to life. I knew something had to change.

In our second year of ministry at the church, I had the privilege to attend a vision trip with Convoy of Hope's Feed One Initiative to Haiti. Our group flew in a day early to spend some time deep sea fishing and relaxing to get away momentarily from the pressures of ministry. Little did I know that this trip would be life-changing for me personally and for our church. Chris Sonksen was the guide for the trip. My first memory of our interaction was driving to dinner in Miami, FL, after a day of fishing and listening to him sing "Copa Cabana" in between intermittent questions about who we were and where we pastored. His singing quickly broke the ice with our group!

As we laughed through the spontaneous singing moments, Chris took the time to hear our stories and ask questions about our churches. As he listened to our stories, he began to share his vision of coaching pastors to help rescue churches. As I heard his vision to help pastors, hope erupted in my heart! I thought this was precisely what was missing in my church! I did not know how to connect the leadership dots. My lack of experience had caused me to become hesitant in leading the church. Hesitancy, in turn, made the church suffer. During our car ride to eat, Chris made a statement that has stuck with me to this day. Amateurs learn by trial and error; professionals get coaching.

That one statement summed up how I felt—like an amateur. At this point, the thought of remaining a small church had crept in. Thoughts like "maybe church growth isn't for everybody" began to permeate my thinking. I even used the parable of the talents to justify a lack of growth and development. I must be the guy that only had one talent and not enough education. The challenges created uncertainty in my leadership. The more I dwelt on the thoughts, the greater the voices of doubt became. I became unsure if I had what it took to succeed. Slowly, comparison and insecurity subtly crept into my heart, robbing me of confidence.

> Not only did he see the mess, but he also helped me begin cleaning it up!

When Chris shared the passionate mission of Church Rescue, it jolted my thinking! Hearing about the opportunity to receive coaching sparked hope. For the first time as a senior pastor, I felt a sense of assurance that things could get on the right track. A few months after our trip, Chris spoke at our network's annual Men's Conference. During the conference, the opportunity came to sign up for coaching. I couldn't get my phone out fast enough to scan the QR code on the screen. I hurriedly filled out the information needed and hit send. That moment marked the beginning of change. Shortly after the conference, I received an email to set up my first coaching call with Chris.

Reviving the Church in America

Leading up to my first call, I had mixed emotions. On the one hand, I was extremely excited about the opportunity; on the other, I was afraid. The thoughts of doubt began to permeate my mind when I realized someone with experience was about to see behind the veil of my leadership. Would they think I was a poor leader? Would they still want to coach me when they saw the good, the bad, and the ugly? That may sound a bit outrageous, but I had a genuine concern. Thankfully, the connection to a coach proved to be a game-changer. Not only did he see the mess, but he also helped me begin cleaning it up! Initially, I was concerned that the coaching process would train us to duplicate someone else's church. I did not want to become a copy and paste of another church. My experience was the polar opposite, as the heart of the coaching propelled us to become who God made us to be, not a cookie-cutter church. We identified where we were on the life-cycle of a church. We found our weak spots and began to work towards solutions. If I were to sum up in one word how I felt after all the initial coaching sessions, it would be traction. We began to see small victories in many areas! Coaching was the key to opening new levels of understanding that helped us stop spinning our wheels.

JOEL WOOD

The Bible tells us in Proverbs 4:7 (NKJV), "Wisdom is the principal thing; Therefore get wisdom. And in all your getting, get understanding."

In leadership, wisdom comes from those who have it. To receive it will require humility and seeking. God had given leaders to equip us, but we had to seek their counsel and be willing to listen. I have learned through the coaching process that wisdom is more significant than knowledge. It is possible to gain knowledge about leadership and yet still cannot lead. It is another thing to utilize the knowledge you have gained and put it into practice to produce results. A person with wisdom has the ability and capacity to activate and apply knowledge.

For example, I know an airplane can fly, but I do not know how to fly it. A pilot also understands that an aircraft can fly, but they have the wisdom to fly the airplane. They know what every knob and instrument is for. They know how to achieve lift, keep the aircraft flying, and, more importantly, land safely. Their wisdom allows people to move from one place to another safely. The beauty of the analogy is that anyone can learn to become a pilot if they go to flight school. It is not that pilots were born to fly; they were instructed on how to do it. They chose close proximity to instructors to gain knowledge and understanding of how to fly.

Coaching was the key that unlocked knowledge and understanding. Areas of our ministry that seemed stuck began to gain traction and momentum. I remember on one early coaching call, Chris was sharing that vision leaks and people drift. I responded to him by asking, "What do you do when the primary leader is the one leaking and drifting?" After a good laugh, he shared how important it was to have a clear vision and defined values. It would be unkind to my team to be unclear as the leader. I understood the knowledge he gave but underestimated the process, time, and energy it would take to create clarity. Thankfully, Chris patiently walked me through the process of how to do it. Here are a few key things that have resonated most with me.

1. There wasn't anything wrong with my church or people. There was something wrong with my thinking.

Craig Groschel, the lead pastor of Life Church, has forbidden his church staff from speaking this statement: *"My people won't."* I found myself riddled with this type of thinking. My people won't lead. My people won't engage. My people won't invite people. Chris taught me that people would follow a clear, compelling vision. The problem was not with the people; it was me. Once I owned up to that, I could get my eyes off people and onto the mission. Gaining clarity of mission gave us the ability to move forward more efficiently. Leadership decisions became more streamlined because we had clearly defined who we were and what we do.

The potential of the church hinges on my willingness to grow. John Maxwell said it best, "Everything rises and falls on leadership."[12] Learning to change my thought process has changed our church. Early in the coaching, it took me a fair amount of time to grasp the concepts I was learning. I needed them to become second nature. Through continued coaching, much of what I have learned is now part of who I am as a leader. There is always more to learn, but I am thankful for how much has changed.

As a former athlete, many habits had to become second nature. In basketball, I couldn't look at the ball while I dribbled. In football, I had to memorize the playbook through repetition. In my senior year, we ran a triple-read option offense. The success of the offense rested on my ability to read the defense. I couldn't guess

---

[12] John Maxwell, "Everything rises and falls on leadership," *BrainyQuote*, https://www.brainyquote.com/quotes/john_c_maxwell_600859.

what they were going to do. I had to play after play and read the defense end. Training in the offseason had to be intense to be successful. Leading a staff was the same. Consistent training, attention to detail, and repetition were needed for us to succeed.

2. Stick with it!

I will shoot straight with you. We could be further down the road if I had stuck with it more consistently early on. From experience, I know that coaching works. The principles you learn from coaching cohorts work. Instead of digging in, I became disillusioned with certain areas and backed off—allowing personal frustration, excuses, and staff to talk me out of what I knew was right. Decide to fight through those moments and push on. Good things will await you on the other side of consistency. Let my failure be your encouragement. Don't give up prematurely.

I have now been receiving coaching for almost six years. In the past two years, we expanded the coaching opportunity to our staff. Our church has grown from thirty to over 300. Like many other churches, our attendance plummeted after COVID. We had lost roughly 50 percent of our people, and after several attempts to connect, it was clear they were not coming back. Within the first twelve months following COVID, my entire staff had changed. What did we do? We got back to work! We stepped right back into what we had been taught. We found the right people and put them in the right seats. We are relentlessly pursuing our mission. The result is growth and life change.

I believe we are just getting started. We have a clearly defined mission and established core values. We have developed a strategy to accomplish the church's mission. We know how to measure wins and put people in the right seats. We have identified and diligently worked to establish the culture that we desire. Our weekly services are more engaging. We have seen more salvations, healings, and baptisms in the past twelve months than in the previous three years, and now we are working to develop a leadership pipeline. Coaching has given us the tools to grow personally and corporately.

To see where we are today is humbling. The church has regained health in every area! The power of the gospel is transforming lives! The fulfillment of your vision is possible. Find a coach. I promise you won't regret it!

The Sleeping Giant

In the first two years of Church Rescue, hundreds of pastors and their churches have seen dramatic progress. Pastors have restored vision, leaders have more confidence, and churches are growing again. Healthy churches are getting involved in the movement, and I believe they are the sleeping giant that's awakening all across our land. Business leaders who hear about Church Rescue are giving generously to this cause because they know that America depends on strong churches to be the backbone of our morality, integrity, and growth. Some of these corporate CEOs and presidents may not be believers, but they know that if we lose churches, we lose the America they love.

Magazine editors are calling us because they heard what we're doing. The conversation often goes something like this:

"So... you're coaching these pastors for free?"

Reviving the Church in America

"Yes."

"And you're providing financial resources so they can be more attractive to people in their communities?"

"Uh-huh."

"The sponsoring churches are donating thousands of dollars in resources?"

"That's right."

"Are you going to charge them later?"

"No, it's entirely free."

"And on top of that, you're paying for a four-day spiritual refreshment retreat for these pastors?"

"Exactly."

"So, what's the secret sauce?"

"There's no secret sauce. We've just identified a huge need and invited people to join us in meeting

THE SLEEPING GIANT

it. And they're being more generous than I could have imagined!"

Today, we have forty coaches, each leading eight to ten pastors. We aren't focused on any denomination. As pastors tell their friends, leaders from many different Christ-centered faith traditions have asked for our help.

We're facing a crisis of faith and truth that is unparalleled in our history. Sociologists and research centers have identified an insidious trend that threatens the foundation of our faith and our culture. Throughout our country (more prevalent among the younger generation but throughout all age groups), people have adopted a worldview called "moralistic therapeutic deism" (MTD). It's *moralistic* because these people, including many who attend church, believe in the inherent goodness of people, and the goal is to be good to each other. They don't believe people are sinful and need a Savior—they believe "good people" go to heaven. It's *therapeutic* because the second goal is to have a happy life. They don't believe in absolute truths or that God has a higher purpose for them. It's a form of *deism* because they believe God may have somehow spun the universe into existence, but he remains distant and unknowable. He's little more than an afterthought. George Barna

Reviving the Church in America

created the *American Worldview Inventory 2021* and concluded that moralistic therapeutic deism is "fake Christianity", even though many of them call themselves Christians. He elaborates:

> *Young adults have grown up with a culturally adulterated version of the Christian faith. They have adopted a softer, twisted version of genuine Christianity. The good news is practitioners of MTD are not anti-religion or anti-Christianity. They just are not willing to surrender themselves to authentic Christianity's demands—or to believe that a real faith would even make such demands of them.*

> *The fact that a greater percentage of people who call themselves Christian draw from MTD than they do from the Bible says a lot about the state of the Christian Church in America—in all of its manifestations. Simply and objectively stated, Christianity in this nation is rotting from the inside out.*[13]

I'm alarmed at this growing threat to the church, but it doesn't do any good to sit back and lament that "the

---

13 George Barna, "American Worldview Inventory 2021", *Arizona University Cultural Research Center*, 13 April 2021, https://www.arizonachristian.edu/wp-content/uploads/2021/05/CRC_AWVI2021_Release01_Digital_01_20210413.pdf.

THE SLEEPING GIANT

church is rotting from the inside out." When we see the problem, we need to take action. Church Rescue is more than a good idea; it's a powerful movement of God to change the culture of America "one saved disciple at a time".

About eighteen months ago, I met a pastor at a conference where he heard me speak. At the time, about thirty people attended his church each Sunday. He described the challenges he faced, and after a long silence, he looked at me and said, "Chris, I can't do this any longer. It's over for me. Our church is about to close. I'm such a failure."

I told him I'd stick with him, and together, we'd trust God to rescue his church. I had time in my schedule a few weeks later, so I offered to visit with him. He shook his head and told me, "I can't pay for your flight, and I can't pay for a hotel."

I responded, "That's okay. It's on me."

When we met at his church, his mood hadn't changed much. His church was barely hanging on, and it wouldn't last much longer. I met with him and a couple of his volunteers, and we created a strategy to turn things around.

Reviving the Church in America

Over the following year, the pastor and I talked on Zoom every month about his spiritual health, how to lead well, and new strategies he might employ to grow the church. I spoke at his church recently. There were over 300 people in the congregation—in a building that had looked like a group of ants in an airplane hangar only eighteen months before! As I met person after person, they told me how the pastor and others at the church had led them to Christ, baptized them, and helped them keep their families together. Many of them were involved in community outreach programs that provide resources for hungry kids, senior adults, teenagers, and people who struggle with addictions. The pastor told them I'd been of some help, so they all thanked me. More than one person said, "If it wasn't for you and Church Rescue, we wouldn't be here."

When the service was done and I walked out with the pastor, he turned to me and said, "Chris, no one has ever believed in me like you do." That sentence means more than he'll ever know.

One of my favorite scenes in the gospels is in Luke's account. Jesus was preaching at the water's edge at the Sea of Galilee, and he noticed two fishing boats nearby. He asked Peter, the owner of one of the boats, to push

THE SLEEPING GIANT

it out into the water and let him preach from it so the people on the shore could hear better. Luke brings us to that moment:

> *When he had finished speaking, he said to Simon [Peter], "Put out into deep water, and let down the nets for a catch." Simon answered, "Master, we've worked hard all night and haven't caught anything. But because you say so, I will let down the nets." When they had done so, they caught such a large number of fish that their nets began to break. So they signaled their partners in the other boat to come, and they came and fill both boats so full that they began to sink.* —Luke 5:4-7

Peter had fished all night and caught nothing. I'm sure he had plenty of reasons to turn Jesus down, but he said, "But if you say so," and he responded. He committed to do what Jesus told him to do, even though it made little sense, even though he was dead tired, and even though it could have made him look foolish to the other fishermen watching this discussion. That's our hearts' response to God's direction to start Church Rescue. We didn't know it would work (or if it would work), we didn't see how we'd find all the resources, and we didn't know if we'd look foolish to people who were watching us. We just heard Jesus give us the instruction to take a step of faith to help pastors of struggling churches, and each of us said, "I'm in."

The second insight we can apply is that Peter shouted to his partners to help him because he couldn't handle the blessing by himself. There were so many fish that the nets were tearing, and he was losing fish. He needed their help, and they gladly participated in the miracle.

That's the essence of Church Rescue: we're just following Jesus's command, and we're inviting people to join us in the miracle of seeing churches turned around for the glory of God and the impact on their communities.

To fulfill the vision and see churches thrive, we need ongoing partners who pray for us, give as much as they can to the movement (go to churchboom.org), and tell others to become partners, too. We can't do it alone. The problem is too big, the need is too great, the stakes are too high. . . . we need your help.

www.ingramcontent.com/pod-product-compliance
Lightning Source LLC
Chambersburg PA
CBHW050912160426
43194CB00011B/2374